Revised Edition

TRANSITIONS ACROSS CULTURES

A Guide to Culture Shock for Travelers
and Those Who Love Them

STEPHEN W. JONES

Copyright © 2020 Stephen W. Jones

All rights reserved. No part of this book may be reproduced, stored in a retrieval system, or transmitted, in any form or by any means, electronic, mechanical, photocopying, recording, or otherwise, without the prior written permission of the Publisher.

Book Cover and Layout by Najdan Mancic
Graphics by Philip McBride and Najdan Mancic
Paris illustration by fruitful design: **www.fruitful-design.com**

The Practical Interculturalist® is a registered mark of Excegent Communication, LLC.

Paperback: ISBN-13: 978-1-940105-05-5
eBook: ISBN-13: 978-1-940105-06-2
Kindle: ISBN-13: 978-1-940105-07-9

The Practical Interculturalist
An Imprint of Excegent Communication, LLC
Watertown, MN
www.thepracticalinterculturalist.com

This book is designed to provide information for our readers. It is provided with the understanding that neither the author nor the publisher is engaged to render any type of psychological, legal, or any other kind of professional advice. The publisher and the individual author shall not be liable for any physical, psychological, emotional, financial, or commercial damages. The publisher and author do not assume and hereby disclaim any liability to any party for any loss, damage, or disruption caused by errors or omissions, whether such errors or omissions result from negligence, accident, or any other cause.

We may earn a commission from purchases made through some of the websites/links included in this book. Some links go to the publisher's web pages and some to other companies' product pages. We actively manage these links and their destinations may change from time to time. Our interest is providing you the best quality information either directly or through referral to a high-quality resource.

DEDICATION

This book is dedicated to those who choose sojourn to make the world a better place, and to those who have to sojourn because it isn't.

CONTENTS

Preface to the Revised Edition 1

Acknowledgements 5

CHAPTER ONE: *Why This Book?* 7

CHAPTER TWO: *What Is Culture?* 15

CHAPTER THREE: *The Process of Transition* 35

CHAPTER FOUR: *Culture Shock* 51

CHAPTER FIVE: *Preparing for Cross-Cultural Success* .. 69

CHAPTER SIX: *Coming Home and Welcoming Back* .. 97

CHAPTER SEVEN: *Parting Words* 111

Glossary 119

Additional Resources 129

References 131

About the Author 135

PREFACE

REVISED EDITION

The original edition of *Transitions Across Cultures* was intended to fill a gap. Over and over again, I came across people who should have known about the principles presented in the book but had no real grasp of them. It has been seven years since I first wrote the book, and both research[1] and practical experience since then have continued to point to the importance of the subject.

Both sojourners and their family members have confirmed to our team that this book was uniquely useful to them. They have told us that having the simple frameworks this book makes available close at hand has helped them unravel some of their own interior mystery and to sort out the relational and practical difficulties connected to transitions.

I think we can always improve. In this edition, I have made the underlying source material more accessible. Combined with *The Practical Interculturalist's* growing web presence and teaching aids, I think this revised edition will help sojourners and their friends and families to continue to grow in their practical understanding of the topics at hand.

I have also tried to provide clarity around the difficult issues of mental health throughout the book. This is a difficult issue and I wrestled with whether to include it at all. I decided to keep the language related to mental health because on balance, I would rather acknowledge that the stresses of culture shock can be psychologically disturbing than pretend that this isn't the case. I am not a mental health professional and do not pretend to be one.

All I can do is what I do when I meet with people in person—encourage you to consider the question of whether you might need to seek professional mental health support. Sometimes I have literally walked with people to the counseling office to set up their first appointment as they have asked for help overcoming their fears. That is more than I can do for you, for obvious reasons. Not everyone needs to meet with a counselor, but it is important that we destigmatize both the presence of mental health challenges and the important help offered by qualified therapists.

My profound hope for you, the reader, is that the cross-cultural transition that inspired you to acquire this book (whether the transition is yours or a loved one's) will be rewarding and successful. Great things can come from cross-cultural transitions, but they are almost never easily attained. The team at *The*

Practical Interculturalist will continue developing resources to attempt to serve you better.

With love, hope, and admiration for the millions who are crossing cultures every day.

STEPHEN JONES,
December 2019, Minnesota

NOTES

[1] Furnham, A. (2019). Culture Shock: A Review of the Literature for Practitioners. *Psychology*, *10*, 1832

ACKNOWLEDGEMENTS

I am grateful to Jennie, to my colleagues, and to you, the readers who make this work both necessary and possible.

CHAPTER ONE

WHY THIS BOOK?

Every year, millions of people are engaged in cultural transition. Study abroad students and facilitators, international students, missionaries, Peace Corps Volunteers, global service-learners, international businesspeople and business travelers, refugees, asylum seekers, asylees, economic migrants, aid and development workers, military members, and trailing spouses and third-culture kids are all undergoing cross-cultural transitions every day.

Unfortunately, many people are underprepared for the disruptions caused by these transitions. For some the consequences are relatively minor—culture shock may be experienced as an inconvenience, or as L. Robert Kohls called it "the occupational hazard of overseas living."[2] For others, however, the consequences of culture shock can be profound and have lasting impacts on their lives. At the least, people who are unprepared for culture shock are likely to be unable to make the most of their experiences. Many people have a vague sense that they have not gotten all they could out of their cultural exchange, and some are left with a lasting inability to integrate valuable lessons into their life. However, for others the disorientation caused by culture shock can give rise to relational, career, and health challenges and breakdowns of either short or long-term duration. Major decisions people make during periods of culture shock can irrevocably impact their lives.

The results of poor preparation for cultural transition can be stark. Moreover, this disorientation continues, often unexpectedly, if and when people return home. Lack of proper reintegration can result in lost productivity, unplanned vocational changes, and broken relationships. Cultural transitions are so potentially disruptive that some have observed that mental illness can result from cultural transitions that are not fully or properly processed.[3]

There is good news, however. When sojourners effectively prepare for and engage in cultural transitions, the results can be phenomenally good. Broadened perspectives, increased creative capacity, and expanded networks can result from well-managed cultural transitions. Preparation alone is not a cure-all; nearly everyone who enters deeply into another culture will experience culture shock. This does not diminish with age or prior experience.[4] However, it is possible to better prepare yourself to navigate the transition, and even just understanding the transitional experience can be helpful to overcoming its worst effects.

WHY I WROTE THIS BOOK

I have been personally involved in cultural transitions since the 1980s, when I was growing up as the son of a naval officer. The first transition I remember was from Virginia to Texas. I began kindergarten there, and my memory is that Texas does a great job of instilling the love of the place in young children. But after two years in Texas public schools, we were headed off to Japan. I remember looking at books from the library with my mom and sister and being not only bewildered but terrified about this strange and faraway place.

Japan ended up being a wonderful place to live, but between the death of my grandfather shortly after we moved, my dad's long deployments including Desert Shield and Desert Storm, and the Mt. Pinatubo eruption in the Philippines, I was ready to return to the US in fourth grade.

Coming back to the US was good but very hard. We lived in southern California for about nine months and then headed to Kansas. In a situation to which many military brats and TCKs can relate, I was in three different schools my fourth-grade year, each in vastly different places.

It wasn't until I was working on my master's degree that I really discovered the principles of culture shock, reentry, and what the third-culture kid is. I repeatedly called my sister with new insights: "I just found out why we were so messed up!"

After studying in Mexico for six months as part of a global service-learning program in college, I decided to go into higher education. Since 2004, I have been working with college students in various stages of cultural transition as well. I have worked with students preparing to study in Asia, Europe, Latin America, and Africa. I have traveled with and been responsible for students in Africa and Latin America, as well as in various regions in the US, including on an Indian Reservation in South Dakota, in the Deep South, and in the Pacific Northwest. I have also worked with international students studying in the US.

I also have worked with international non-profit organizations. Each year the position at my college most closely related to mine is filled by a couple on a one-year home assignment. This is my seventh year in this role, and I have had the opportunity to watch 14 of my colleagues up close in the two semesters of collaboration we have while they are in the midst of transitions. In my work teaching, I have had the opportunity to visit others abroad and often to observe and sometimes coach people in the midst of different stages of transition.

My wife Jennie and I have also had the privilege of debriefing groups of "first-term returners" who are living in the US for a year for the first time after four or five years abroad. Jennie and I have debriefed both students and career professionals who are in the midst of transitions.

One of the most unfortunate things I have observed in all of this is how few people are well prepared for cross-cultural transitions. I have seen, in my own students, the difference in success between students who are well prepared and those who aren't. I have also seen tremendous differences between those who recognize the realities of culture shock and reentry and those who are unaware of the effects of these phenomena. Without a doubt, those who understand why culture shock happens and how to deal with it are better adapted in the long run. Unprocessed culture shock seems to have a way of lingering—the buried discomforts don't ever really go away. Sometimes, they strike back with a vengeance, like an unattended splinter left to fester. Other times, people are successful at building walls of separation between those disruptive experiences and their present selves, but at the cost of cutting off a very real (and often vibrant) part of their lived experience.

Despite all this, there are still too many schools, businesses, and organizations that don't take seriously how disruptive culture shock can be. I have written and revised this book for three purposes. The *first*, and most immediate, is to enable the people actually traveling to understand what they can expect and how to cope with the disorientation caused by cross-cultural transitions. This includes sojourners who are already well beyond the opportunity to "prepare" but are trying to understand what has happened or what is currently happening in their transition. The *second* purpose is to enable those who are responsible for travelers to understand the seriousness of the cross-cultural transition so they can make appropriate decisions about supporting these individuals. The *third* purpose is to enable supporters of travelers, such as parents, friends, and loved ones, to understand what the traveler is experiencing so they can provide better support.

WHAT TO EXPECT IN THIS BOOK

This short book is intended to enable sojourners, the people responsible for them, and those who love them to better prepare for, process, and reintegrate following cultural transitions. This book is intentionally concise, designed to provide the basic principles for successfully navigating intercultural transitions. This book is *not* about how to effectively communicate across cultures. I have included a list of recommended resources at the end to help in that regard.

To accomplish the goal of doing transition better, each chapter of this book contains a mixture of intercultural theory and examples. Finally, readers can expect to find specific guidelines for engaging the transition, as well as practical tips on how to make the most of applying the theory.

Bolded words can be found in the glossary for clarification.

DISCLAIMER

Although this book is definitely intended to assist you in your journey, each person's experience is necessarily different. Some of the ideas here may apply to you (or your family, friends, employees, etc.), while others may not. These are suggested as hypotheses, to be held openly in your hand. If these tools fit, great! If they don't, don't try to force them to work—there may be something else going on. As per usual in a book like this, any advice given should not be interpreted as medical, psychological, or other professional advice. Don't use this book to replace your need for the help and support of competent professionals!

NOTES

[2] Kohls, L. R. (2001). *Survival kit* for *overseas living: For Americans planning to live and work abroad* (4th ed). London: Published by Nicholas Brealey Pub. in association with Intercultural Press, Yarmouth, Maine. More at: https://survivalkit.traxcultures.com

[3] Lucas, J. (2009). Over-stressed, Overwhelmed, and Over Here: Resident Directors and the Challenges of Student Mental Health Abroad. *Frontiers: The Interdisciplinary Journal of Study Abroad*, XVIII, 187–216.

[4] For a review of literature that includes a discussion of risk factors for culture shock, see Furnham, A. (2019). Culture Shock: A Review of the Literature for Practitioners. *Psychology*, *10*, 1832. https://doi.org/10.4236/psych.2019.1013119

CHAPTER TWO

WHAT IS CULTURE?

CONCEPT 1

Culture is the way people do life together

Countless definitions exist for culture, but for the purpose of this book, we are really interested in exploring **culture** as *the way groups of people do life together*. Think about it this way: What makes your family different than your best friend's family? What makes your city or town different from the next city or town up the road? What makes Florida different from New Mexico? What makes Holland different from Sri Lanka? In each case, there are certain patterns of how the groups of people do life together. These patterns are influenced by everything from geography to climate to religion to patterns of commerce, and more!

The challenge with culture is that not all of these patterns are readily visible. One of the popular illustrations of culture is the comparison to an iceberg. The basic idea is that while certain elements of culture are readily visible at the top of the iceberg, such as clothing and food, the majority of culture is actually below the surface, making it more difficult to see, understand, and relate to.

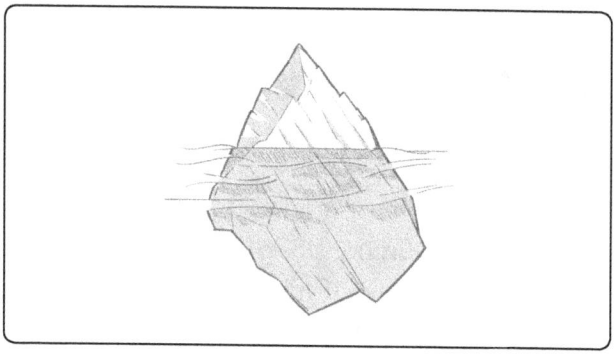

So what makes up the bottom of the iceberg? At this level, you find values and beliefs that both undergird the visible behaviors and are shaped by them. For example, a culture that highly values competitiveness may demonstrate this through external behaviors like youth club sports. Of course, culture is not *an iceberg*.[5] Specifically, the danger of thinking of culture as an iceberg is that it might lead us to think of culture as some kind of static entity. Culture is not so much a *thing* as it is a *process*.[6] But, the important point here is that while much of culture is visible to us, much more is invisible.

CONCEPT 2

Cultures are often (very) different from each other

If culture is how people do life together, then we are able to rely on culture to provide written and unwritten rules about how life works. Our cultures tell us how to greet people, what makes a good job candidate, how to interview, and how to express confidence and respect.[7] We usually learn all of these things without ever having to read books on etiquette. Our cultures also tell us what success looks like, and they instill deep values about the relationship between people and task. What might be most important is that culture forms in us the crucial skill of recognizing and utilizing common sense.

The challenge is that cultural patterns are doing this same thing—teaching common sense—for someone from another part of town or another part of the planet. But, it's happening differently. What my culture has decided looks like respect might look like arrogance in someone else's culture. Our cultures might define a successful job candidate in different, or even opposite, ways. Just imagine how different common sense could look. For example, in the culture I currently live in, it is usually appropriate to look someone else in the eyes to show genuineness. Yet there are cultures in which eye contact is a sign of disrespect. If you and I have a conversation in which I keep looking into your eyes and you keep looking down, what a terribly confusing conversation we could have! If we come from cultures with different respect strategies, you and I might both feel disrespected precisely because we were both trying to show respect to the other! And not only that, but my friends would know that I was doing it right because it's just *common sense* that looking in someone's eyes shows respect. Yet your friends would also know that you were doing it right because it's just *common sense* that looking down shows deference.

CONCEPT 3

It's more complicated than we think it is

The following conversation between a teacher and his students exemplifies the use of cultural shortcuts in everyday life. The teacher starts by asking the students to describe this object:

What Is Culture? | 19

More about this image at: https://stoplight.traxcultures.com

Teacher: *What do you see?*

Student: *It's a stoplight!*

Teacher: *What do you see?*

Student: *A traffic signal!*

Teacher: *What do you see?*

Student: *A rectangular box with three circular lights—yellow, red, and green!*

Teacher: *What do you see?*

Student: *A drawing of a stoplight?*

Teacher: *Okay, now we're getting somewhere. What do you see in the drawing?*

Student: *Well, it looks like a rectangle, but it isn't quite, and your circles are drawn badly.*

Teacher: *Great, so you see a drawing of something kind of like a rectangle, with three badly drawn circles of different colors? Is that what everyone would see looking at this?*

Student: *Well, yeah, unless they were color blind.*

Teacher: *Okay, so would that change the color of the drawing?*

Student: *Well . . . kind of, but no, it doesn't. But it changes the way the person would see the drawing.*

Teacher: *Interesting. Tell me what the drawing means to you.*

Student: *Well, it's a stoplight for directing traffic.*

Teacher: *Okay, what do the different lights mean?*

Student: *Green means go, red means stop, and yellow means slow down.*

Teacher: *Are you sure that's what those mean? Let's take green, for example. What does it really mean?*

Student: *So you're saying it doesn't mean go? Hmm ... Well, I guess it means proceed through the intersection if conditions are safe.*

Teacher: *That seems like a good bet. I'm going to suggest that red doesn't really mean stop. What do you think it means?*

Student: *Maybe that we shouldn't go through the intersection. Unless we're already in the intersection when it turns red, in which case we should get out right away. Or unless we stop first and make a right-hand turn. Or, if we're at the intersection of two one-way streets, it might be possible to turn left, but you have to stop first.*

Teacher: *Okay, good. So what you're saying is that it's complicated?*

Student: *Yeah. And yellow means Speed Up!*

Teacher: *Or, more precisely, it means . . .*

Student: *I think it means make up your mind on how to be safe. Either get through the intersection or stop before you enter the intersection.*

This little dialogue illustrates that we take a lot of things for granted. We constantly use shortcuts to make life around us easier to understand. We see a drawing and interpret it as a stoplight. Of course it isn't; it's a drawing. (And we can get more complicated here—we're actually interpreting light reflecting off pigments; the pigments are actually absorbing all the colors except the ones we see; not everyone's eyes and brains interpret colors the same way, etc.) We see a red light and say, "Oh, that means 'stop,'" but of course, that isn't what it really means. And yet we are largely able to function without talking about what red really means because, as a culture, we have stored that information as **tacit knowledge**. We don't have to think about it.

SO LET'S RECAP WHAT WE KNOW SO FAR.

- **Concept 1:** Culture is the way people do their stuff together.

- **Concept 2:** Cultures are often (very) different from each other.

- **Concept 3:** It's more complicated than we think it is.

These lead us to Concept 4:

CONCEPT 4

Moving between cultures is deeply disorienting

If we recognize that culture is the way people do life together, that people do life in very different ways from each other, and that much of this is happening in our subconscious, it shouldn't be surprising that moving between cultures can be deeply disorienting.

••

Imagine that you have grown up in a culture where you start the day at around 7 o'clock. This shouldn't be too difficult for most American readers. You have your coffee, grab a bite to eat, and head to work. What time do you eat lunch? Around 12 o'clock is an approximate guess, and you probably wrap up your workday around 5 or 6 o'clock. Pretty straightforward, right?

Now imagine that you find yourself in a culture where a business associate asks you to meet him at 6 o'clock for a meal on Tuesday. Tuesday comes, and you go through the workday looking forward to the evening meal. You show up at the restaurant at the appointed time, but your host doesn't show up. After a long and awkward period of drinking soda and waiting, you finally decide to head home, disappointed and hurt. The next day, your would-be host mentions that he was disappointed that you didn't join him yesterday, and could you reschedule for the following week?

What's happened? There are at least three possibilities. Really, there are hundreds, but we'll take three. Oftentimes in cross-cultural situations, the first possibility that comes to our minds is negative, and often it is about the other person. Even if we don't normally assume the worst about people, we tend to misattribute behaviors we don't understand to bad character. In this case, for example, you might be likely to think that your host is not being totally straightforward in the relationship, or that he's at least not totally honest. After all, why can't he just admit that he forgot, instead of blaming you? Even though this seems like a very negative reaction, it is a surprisingly common one.

The second possibility is that you simply didn't wait long enough. In some cultures, times are simply ballpark estimates. Perhaps your host showed up at 8 o'clock, and he was surprised to find that you did not come. He might have been shocked to imagine that you were in fact there but had already left.

A third possibility is that you were late! In Ethiopia, for example, 6 o'clock falls closer to the middle of the day than to the end of it. What Americans would call 7 o'clock in the morning is called 1:00 daylight. Thus, noon, when the sun is at the highest point overhead, occurs around 6 o'clock rather than 12. So, if you might have been there at 7 o'clock, you might have been about six hours late!

••

The point of this section is not to consider different ways that time is understood in different cultures, but rather to demonstrate the real differences in perspective that are possible across cultures. These striking differences are found not just in relation to time but across all areas of what it means to be human, and even in relation to fundamental questions about the substance of reality! In each case, most of the differences are primarily acknowledged in our tacit awareness, rather than overtly.

When we cross cultures, we carry with us a kind of internal guide-map of how life works. In that map, we carry critical information like how to make friends; how to provide for our basic necessities like food, shelter, and using the toilet; and how to be successful. These basic things are normally quite natural for adults by the time we are engaging in cultural sojourns, whether as students, business travelers, missionaries, or Peace Corps volunteers. We have successfully built our map of how the world works using the cultural patterns we have grown up with. This is also the case for **third-culture kids** and **global nomads**, although it plays out somewhat differently. So, when we enter another culture and begin to figure out how to do life, we are already using a (subconscious) map that we may not be particularly aware of. Remember the iceberg metaphor—most of the substance of a culture may be hidden even to members of a culture!

One reason moving across cultures can be so deeply disorienting is that our map is often *wrong* in this new setting. Certain paths or roads look familiar, so we try to orient our map according to them, only to find out that they lead to places we weren't looking to go.

A friend of mine who came to the US for college as an international student told the humorous story of how he missed breakfast his first day at school because he could not figure out how to exit the building. He explained that "Your exits are not exits!" When leaving the dorm, he thought he was not supposed to take the elevator in case there was a fire (the sign read: "DO NOT TAKE ELEVATOR IN CASE OF FIRE"). In his culture, hardly any such signs existed, so he assumed there must be a very high risk of fire for people who took the elevator. So, instead he would take the stairs down to the lowest level. There are almost no basements in his home country, so he expected that the lowest level would lead him outside. First floor, to him, meant the first elevated floor, or what Americans call the second floor.

As he took the stairs all the way down, he found himself in the building's basement. He wandered around looking for an exit but could not find one. So, he went to turn around and go back out the door to the stairwell that he had just come through. However, there was a sign on it that said "FIRE DOOR, KEEP CLOSED." Again, such signs were incredibly rare in his country, and he grew increasingly concerned about the possibility of fire.

Then he saw a sign instructing its readers to run clockwise on Mondays, Wednesdays, and Fridays and to run counterclockwise on Tuesdays, Thursdays, and Saturdays. Not realizing that he had stumbled onto the college's running track in the building's basement, he thought these signs were because of the risk of fire, so he started to run! He kept finding doors that said things he didn't understand (like "emergency exit, alarm will sound"), and it took two increasingly frantic hours before he found a way out of the building!

My friend laughs about this experience now. However, there are also far less comical circumstances, where the reality of mismatched maps can cause deep disturbances, as **sojourners** find themselves misinterpreted and unable to function or communicate effectively in their new cultural milieu.

Using the wrong cultural map can be deeply disorienting—especially when certain "landmarks" look familiar.[8]

CONCEPT 5

Disorientation caused by crossing cultural barriers can be anticipated and reduced, but not eliminated

A student once told a colleague of mine that she wasn't going to experience **culture shock** because she had never been tired after flying before. Despite his attempts to explain the difference between **jet lag** and culture shock, she entered a six-month sojourn with the idea that once she caught up on her sleep, the worst would be behind her.

This underestimation is unfortunately not limited to new sojourners. I had another student who had grown up as a third-culture kid who was certain that he would not experience culture shock because he had been back and forth between different cultures so many times. This individual had one of the worst cases of culture shock I had seen up to that point, in part because his identity was partly based on being adept at moving between cultures.

I shake my head when I hear seasoned business travelers explain that they never get culture shock. Why? Here's the issue: Nearly everyone who enters deeply into another culture will experience culture shock (no matter how many times he or she has done it before).⁹

There is something about the experience of being human that causes people to be deeply affected when we encounter life that is understood in ways that are very different from what we are used to—even if we already know what to expect in the host culture. A few years ago, a friend of mine who was living internationally remarked to me that she was experiencing one of her most difficult rounds of culture shock. This was after more than two decades of international living! The disruption caused by crossing cultures is not just for the uninitiated.

Through *planning*, *preparation*, and perhaps most importantly, *ongoing reflection*, sojourners can anticipate, reduce the effects of, and more effectively navigate culture shock. However, it cannot be entirely eliminated.

The experience of real cross-cultural difference "always contains an element of violation" when we encounter it up close.[10] This idea, even if it seems fatalistic, must be properly accounted for. The only way to be in another culture and not experience culture shock is to fail to engage deeply with the culture.

MOVING FORWARD

This chapter was designed to provide a brief overview of the realities involved with crossing cultures. The following chapters will deal in depth with ideas that will help you better navigate the sojourn, whether it is your own or that of a friend or family member.

- ▷ **Chapter 3** addresses the process of transition, as applied to the cross-cultural sojourn.

- ▷ **Chapter 4** looks into the unique realities of culture shock and factors that increase the intensity of cross-cultural sojourns.

- ▷ **Chapter 5** explores the preparation for and experience of a cross-cultural sojourn.

- ▷ **Chapter 6** considers the unique challenges facing those who return from a cross-cultural sojourn, including advice for family and friends.

- ▷ **Chapter 7** offers a few concluding thoughts.

You might have noticed that this book does not take a one-sidedly optimistic look at the process of moving across cultures. It may even seem discouraging to people, as a warning against transitioning across cultures. That is certainly not the point or goal of this book. Some of humanity's greatest successes in the coming century will be the result of cross-cultural and trans-national collaborations. Instead of discouraging such interactions, my hope is to communicate the seriousness of cross-cultural transition and to better prepare you for success.

NOTES

[5] Bennett, M. J. (2013, September 28). The ravages of reification: Considering the iceberg and cultural intelligence, Towards de-reifying intercultural competence. Presented at the FILE IV, Colle Val d'Elsa, Italy. Retrieved from http://www.idrinstitute.org/allegati/IDRI_t_Pubblicazioni/77/FILE_Documento_Intercultura_Reification.pdf

[6] Morrison, T., & Conaway, W. A. (2006). Kiss, bow, or shake hands: The bestselling guide to doing business in more than 60 countries (2nd ed). Avon, Mass: Adams Media. More at: https://shakehands.traxcultures.com

[7] Morrison, T., & Conaway, W. A. (2006). Kiss, bow, or shake hands: The bestselling guide to doing business in more than 60 countries (2nd ed). Avon, Mass: Adams Media. More at: https://shakehands.traxcultures.com

[8] Find out more about this image at https://parislasvegas.traxcultures.com

[9] Furnham, A. (2019). Culture Shock: A Review of the Literature for Practitioners. Psychology, 10, 1832. https://doi.org/10.4236/psych.2019.1013119

[10] Hoffman, E. (1990). Lost in Translation: A Life in a New Language. (p. 209-210) Penguin. More at: https://lostintranslation.traxcultures.com

CHAPTER THREE

THE PROCESS OF TRANSITION

To understand the process of experiencing transitions across cultures, it is helpful to step back and look at the process of transition in general first.[11] After all, any cross-cultural transition also includes a host of major life transitions as well. William Bridges suggests that when thinking about transitions, it is useful to consider that transitions begin with an ending (or a whole lot of endings!), rather than with a beginning.[12] On its face, this seems confusing, but it is actually a key perspective for the successful navigation of cultural transitions. The basic process of transition outlined by Bridges is as follows:

Ending → Transition Zone → Beginning

Bridges suggests that transitions begin with an ending and end with a beginning. Perhaps this is not so difficult to understand, although readers are encouraged to read his updated (2004) book for a thorough discussion of the subject. For example, as a caterpillar transforms into a butterfly, it must first end being a caterpillar. It then goes through the chrysalis stage of transition, and it ends the transition with a new beginning as a butterfly. Whether our own transitions will result in anything resembling a butterfly is irrelevant to the question of how transitions occur, but we can hope!

CONCEPT 6

Begin with the endings

Before people embark on a cross-cultural transition, whether into a new culture or into the process of returning home, I challenge them to develop a list of at least five things that are ending in their lives as a result of the upcoming transition. This is quite different from Stephen Covey's principle that highly effective people "begin with the end in mind."[13] Whereas Covey's idea involves the creative imagining of what can be, I am advocating an honest reckoning of what will no longer be.

Some people are more used to thinking in terms of adding to their lives than to taking things away, and this exercise can be challenging for them. The following example might be helpful:

An undergraduate student who travels from the US to Africa for the first time for study abroad might experience the following endings:

- ▷ She will no longer be a person who hasn't been to Africa.

- ▷ She will no longer be a "normal" college student who spends eight semesters on campus.

- ▷ Her status in her friend group will change.

- ▷ If she has been working, she will likely have to quit her job, with no guarantee of getting it back.

- ▷ Some of her ignorance and naiveté will be lost.

On the face of it, these might seem like small or expected changes for someone who has decided to travel internationally. However, these can actually be very disturbing. Perhaps the most potentially traumatic ending listed above is the last one—the loss of ignorance. It can be very troubling to befriend people whose lives are very different from your own, because there are certain things that you simply cannot un-know. This is true whether you are encountering something wonderful—such as the friendship and warmth possible in human relationships—or something terrible, such as the suffering of others.

The process of discovering **endings** is relevant for any kind of cross-cultural sojourn. For businesspeople who are relocating for work, there is another set of endings that might be difficult to recognize before they happen:

- ▷ Your role in local organizations will likely end. Whether clubs, church, politics, or sports associations, it is simply impossible to maintain your local affiliations in the same way when not present.

- ▷ Your influence in your place of work may diminish. Even though overseas assignments can be a significant step up, they rarely bring more direct influence in the day-to-day operations of the office.

- ▷ Some acquaintanceships and friendships will probably end. Or some perceived friends may be revealed to be mere acquaintances. This is often difficult for people to believe in an age of instant global communication. My students have been shocked to find that even being gone for just four to six months can be enough to disrupt friendships that they thought were strong before they left.

▷ Your sense of what is possible will change. Even the introduction of new possibilities is its own kind of ending, as you find out that your former view was too limited, thus ending it.

▷ Your advancement in your organization will often become less straightforward. International assignments complicate advancement within most organizations, largely because organizations are often unable to adequately help their staff reintegrate upon return. The process of reintegration will be discussed in greater detail in Chapter 6.

Of course there are a host of other changes that depend on the length and intensity of a sojourn. It is worth noting that some endings can result even from very short trips abroad. By way of example, it is possible that even a two-week trip abroad could lead to the end of feeling understood by friends and family. Similarly, such trips often lead to the end of certain myopic perspectives. While this can arguably be a good thing, the truth is that these endings carry a cost.

....

On refugees: It is important to note that I have been describing the circumstances of voluntary sojourners. However, there are many people in the world who find themselves in transition who would not have chosen to relocate. It is especially important that refugees (economic, political, disaster, etc) come to terms with the endings in their lives.

It is also imperative that those who serve refugees recognize the endings and losses that refugees have experienced and will continue to experience. Many of these endings do not become apparent immediately, surfacing in waves as life unfolds in their new "home." It is especially important to give space for refugees to mourn these endings, as many of them are absolutely permanent.

....

CONCEPT 7

Engage the transition zone

In developing his model for transitions, Bridges suggested that the middle stage could be called the **transition zone** or the **neutral zone**. For many, the idea that this stage could be called neutral is very troubling, because it is almost always a very difficult stage. I find it helpful to think of this stage as being similar to putting a car into neutral. It doesn't matter how much you press on the accelerator, the vehicle lacks the ability to propel itself while in neutral. This is analogous to many people's experience of being in the midst of a cross-cultural transition.

The sojourner is thrust into the neutral zone by the series of endings just discussed, and these endings can introduce a high level of ambiguity. The sojourner may be stuck thinking, "Well, I'm no longer the way I was, but nothing has replaced that yet." For example, the successful businesswoman who is active in her community may be surprised to find that she is no longer receiving regular praise from those around her. Thus, her status as a force for good in the community is no longer affirmed, causing it, in a sense, to end. Yet, at this point, this status as a force for good has not been replaced by anything. In this in-between state, she is no longer, and also not yet, affirmed as a force for good in the community. This type of disruption is sometimes discussed as **role deprivation**.

The void caused by this in-between space is unsettling for most people; it is also experienced multiple times in various ways in the course of ordinary life. For example, high school graduation or beginning study for a new educational degree, getting married or divorced, gaining or losing a job, the birth of a child or the death of a loved one, are all examples of potentially profound life changes that can provoke the ending / neutral zone experience. Yet in the cross-cultural setting, this transitional phenomena is exacerbated by the mismatched cultural maps described in Chapter 2. For example, the businesswoman mentioned above might find herself unable to quickly replace meaningful community-based friendships due to mismatched cultural patterns surrounding the interplay between work and personal life. Even more frustrating (particularly, but not only, for women) can be mismatched expectations around gender roles, which might lead people to feel unfamiliar and unwelcome restrictions. Add differences around cultural understandings related to time, space, motivation, communication, and nature, and it is easy to see that navigating the transition zone gets a whole lot more complicated when crossing cultures!

The temptation many sojourners face is to rush through the transition zone. This may be particularly so for sojourners with a high value on task and efficiency, or with a strong uncertainty avoidance trait. The discomfort brought on by so much not-knowing and in-between-ness can motivate even very introspective people to try to push past this stage into the new beginnings. Bridges explains that our approach to transition is often like that of crossing a street—only a fool, we reason, would hang out in the middle where it is most dangerous and uncomfortable. Yet transitioning across cultures is not the same as crossing a street.

What I have observed is that those who press *into* the difficulties of the neutral zone are often rewarded in two ways. *First*, they gain tremendous insights into themselves and their own culture that can inspire them for years (or even decades) to come. *Second*, having adequately processed this movement from a kind of death into a kind of rebirth, they encounter far fewer unresolved tensions that unexpectedly flare up well after the transition has been "completed." They seem to be, on the whole, more peaceful. Yet this peace is discovered not by ignoring the difficulties, but rather by intentionally experiencing them.

On the other hand, people who press *through* the transition zone as though it were just a passing cold may rob themselves of some very important information about themselves and their culture. More damaging is the cost of pressing through: certain wounds inflicted by the process (and by people) are allowed to fester—sometimes for years.

This is a most unsatisfactory outcome. I have especially observed this pattern in American missionaries and their families, who often return to the US about once every four years for furlough or home assignment. This time, far from being one of respite, is almost always busier than life in their adoptive country. Through keeping a nearly nonstop schedule of traveling, speaking, conferences, and meetings, missionaries and their families are unfortunately often able to be physically present in the US for a year without ever really processing the transition. This is part of why the third-culture kid mentioned in Chapter 2 had so much difficulty with culture shock. Even though he had been back and forth between different countries for years, he had never been taught how to process the cultural transition.

You might be wondering at this point just how you will be able to successfully navigate the transition zone. Here is a short list of suggested practices:

- ▷ Begin with the endings. Identifying these, and mourning them properly, is really important for healthy transitions.

- ▷ Engage in regular reflection. Guided questions that have been tailored to your situation may be especially helpful.

- ▷ Keep a journal. Journaling is tremendously helpful for successful navigation of cultural differences. Recording events may prove helpful, but one of the most important uses for a journal is the honest assessment of your emotions during the day. Added bonus: Later readings of the journals will often reveal important cultural data that you can't see at the time.

To step it up a notch, create ethnographic fieldnotes.[14]

▷ Don't check out! It is often tempting to check out through media like books and movies, or through communication tools like Facetime, WhatsApp, WeChat, and social media, cell phones, and the internet. Netflix, Disney+, and the like make this even more possible than it used to be. While there is a place for self-care, disappearing from the local context short-circuits the useful process of the neutral zone and can ultimately be self-limiting. Hiding out in the expat community is another mode of checking out that should be avoided.

▷ Do plan for ways that you can cope with the stresses, and allow yourself some (but not too much) downtime. Some access to familiar movies and shows, music, and food can be helpful.

The transition zone is also referred to by Bridges as being like letting land lay fallow. This picture can be useful, because an unplanted field looks to many of us, for all intents and purposes, to be wasted opportunity. However, taking a field out of production for a season may be one of the most beneficial strategies to allow for the longevity of the land. Microbes and fungal networks invisibly revitalize the land as they process the dead residue of the previous year's harvest and turn it into the nutrients that will allow the future harvest to flourish. The picture is apt. The work is happening invisibly, below the surface, and can't be rushed.

CONCEPT 8

Allow the new beginnings to breathe

As the transition process begins to wind down, it is helpful to identify **new beginnings**. It is important not to do this too soon, because the winding nature of the neutral zone may at times fool you into thinking that you're closer to the end of the transition than you actually are. After a while, though, you will likely notice the ambiguity beginning to diminish, and new insights will begin to present themselves. In general, I expect the first two stages of transition to last between six months and two years before sojourners can begin to really see the new beginnings, though of course there is much variation.

Although it may be tempting to rush into new beginnings, premature commitments can cause lasting pain or broken promises. It is often better to be a little bit tentative at this stage. At the same time, this is a wonderful time for exploration of new possibilities. Perhaps the new cultural setting will allow new elements of yourself to come out that you never expected, such as discovering the love of art or cooking, finding a new means of linguistic expression, or finding the seed thoughts for a new business concept.

As these new realities begin to crystallize, you will realize that you are, in some ways, a different version of yourself. This can actually be very frightening to some people, and it is therefore really important to keep track of these new changes. Additionally, some of the new beginnings are new forms of the attributes or circumstances that ended earlier in the transitions. Again, I recommend a journal.

CONCEPT 9

Pick up the thread of continuity

Amidst all of the change experienced in the previous three steps, it might seem like the process of cross-cultural transition involves a complete redefinition of the self. This, fortunately, is not the case. One of Bridges' most important ideas is that of the **thread of continuity**.

Sometime toward the end of the neutral zone (during which it can seem like your whole sense of self is threatened), it becomes easier to see that in spite of all the changes, there is actually a lot that has stayed the same. Not only that, but this is the stage in which it is often possible to identify the most important parts of what you intend to accomplish or be in life. Picking up the thread of continuity is essentially the process of stating to yourself what it was that was true about you before, has been true about you in the transition (even if you forgot), and will be true about you moving forward.

For example, as I moved through the process of transition after losing a job, there came a point when certain themes reemerged, and I saw that in some ways I would be even better able to pursue what I had always cared about. In fact, I realized that the job had actually been preventing me from pursuing some things that were really important to me. Mind you, this insight did not come right away. Still, it is an important step to recognize that at some point in the transition process, you will have the opportunity to pick up the thread of continuity, moving forward with a recognition of who you always have been and who you will be.

Picking up the thread of continuity often involves statements like "Oh yeah, I remember . . ." or "I forgot that I enjoyed this . . .", or "I recall now that I do care about.... How strange to have ever forgotten it!"

While this chapter has dealt with the process of cross-cultural transition, we have only touched on the idea of culture shock. The next chapter will introduce culture shock.

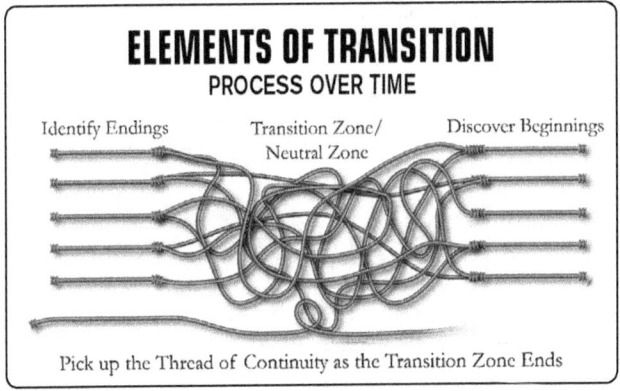

For more on this image, visit https://transitionsprocess.traxcultures.com

NOTES

[11] Some intercultural trainers, such as LaRay Barna, have noted that the study of bereavement may also be an important reference point for understanding cross-cultural transitions. See also Furnham, A., & Bochner, S. (1986). *Culture shock: Psychological reactions to unfamiliar environments.* London ; New York: Methuen.

[12] Bridges, William. (2004). *Transitions: Making sense of life's changes.* (2nd Ed.). Cambridge, MA: DeCapo. More at: https://bridgestransitions.traxcultures.com

[13] Covey, S. R. (2013). *The 7 habits of highly effective people: Powerful lessons in personal change* (25th anniversary edition). New York: Simon & Schuster. More at: https://sevenhabits.traxcultures.com

[14] Emerson, R. M., Fretz, R. I., & Shaw, L. L. (1995). Writing Ethnographic Fieldnotes (1st ed.). University of Chicago Press. Find more at: https://fieldnotes.traxcultures.com

CHAPTER FOUR

CULTURE SHOCK

Culture shock[15] is an idea that is familiar to many people, but I have been surprised by how few actually have some sense of what culture shock is and how to deal with it effectively. I have heard the concept misapplied many times. It should probably be noted at the outset that culture shock, in and of itself, is not a thing that exists in the natural world.[16] It is, instead, a concept used to describe a common pattern experienced by people.

The pattern occurs frequently enough that the concept is useful. However, it is certainly not a natural law, and is also not a disease. When discussing *culture shock* in this chapter, you could substitute the longer (less useful but more accurate) phrase: *the common pattern of disruption, which accompanies cross-cultural transitions, that we call culture shock*. Unwieldy, isn't it? I use the shorter label instead, but recognize that we refer here to a pattern, not a thing.

CONCEPT 10

Culture shock is caused by cumulative disorientation

Culture shock is a response to the **cumulative disorientation** caused by exposure to another culture. This means, for example, that someone who has been in another culture for just one week would not be experiencing culture shock in the way that we are using the idea. It is possible that such a visitor would be experiencing cultural *stress*, but culture shock results from deep and sustained contact with another culture.

Similarly, it is not possible that any single event can cause culture shock. For example, if you were to have a particularly difficult conversation with a member of the host culture, it would not be useful to label that experience as "culture shock." You might be able to call it a cultural clash or cultural miscommunication, but in and of itself the conversation would not be "a culture shock."

As with any popular topic, there are, of course many different ways to approach and define culture shock. In his incredibly useful review of the literature on the subject, Furnham identifies several key features of culture shock. Culture shock:

▷ "is unexpected and surprising"

▷ "is associated with a number of negative emotions."

▷ "leads to an examination of, and attempts to integrate, different understandings of human behaviour."[17]

Furnham argues that culture shock can therefore be defined as a "sudden, unexpected, and surprising set of mainly negative emotions and cognitions associated with encountering a new environment."[18]

It is important to understand culture shock as a cumulative experience, because the isolated events that stand out as being relevant to culture shock will often be confusing on their own. For example, I once had a group of students who said they actually liked having the dirt outside all around them when they first visited a developing nation—there was, they said, something uniquely good about the quality of this red dirt.

Yet within a month of their arrival, these same students had come to loathe the ubiquity of the dirt. It was everywhere—not just on the streets, but in their clothes and beds, on their mangoes, and in their books and computers. In this case, it might be tempting to suggest that the second claim (the bad dirt) is culture shock, whereas the first isn't. In fact—and this is important—*both* of these sentiments are expressions of culture shock. This is in part because both are reactions to sustained contact with unfamiliar stimuli, though taking place at different points of the process. This claim will become more clear in the next section.

In the face of disorientation caused by stimuli such as language, climate, and cultural patterns ranging from hygiene to cuisine to traffic to business and on and on, people go through a somewhat predictable set of steps.

CONCEPT 11

Culture shock follows a relatively predictable pattern

Although culture shock can be a tremendously challenging experience, it does at least tend to follow a predictable series of stages. Familiarity with this pattern can make it easier to navigate successfully. While not everybody experiences the stages in the same way, and not everybody experiences all of them, the general order is 1) emotional high; 2) disenchantment, discouragement, and depression;[19] and 3) confidence and competence.

1) EMOTIONAL HIGH

In many cases, the first stage of culture shock is an **emotional high**. This is not true for everyone, but many people—especially people who have chosen to have the cross-cultural experience—initially feel like being in the new culture is a positive experience. In the first few weeks of a sojourn, it is common for most stimuli to be interpreted through this frame. This is what caused my students to think the dirt was so wonderful.

Importantly, many short-term tourists (or tourists who frequently move from one location to the next) never leave this so-called **honeymoon stage**, leading the majority of tourists who have traveled to think that cultural differences are rather insignificant, and even that such differences are primarily simple and pleasant facts of life. Food, dress, and music are particularly apparent during this stage and are experienced as wonderful. This is the experience of culture that a person might encounter visiting Disney's Epcot center—safe, fascinating, and fun—but it can happen in many different places of the world.

Interestingly, visitors in this stage may rate attributes of the host culture more highly than the actual members of that culture would. This is because the honeymoon stage does not require us to actually understand the other (person, place, thing) in its own context. Additionally, because relational patterns differ across cultures, visitors may wrongly think that they have made closer friends with hosts than is actually the case.

2) DISENCHANTMENT, DISCOURAGEMENT, AND DEPRESSION

The first stage is bound to come to an end because this emotionally high experience of difference cannot be sustained for longer than one or two months. For example, an average American is likely to be overcome by the thought that while it is nice to spend a couple of hours a day socializing over tea, as happens in some West African cultures, it would really be nice to get some tasks done. What at first is a fun curiosity and nice change of pace can eventually become a major irritant.

It is not uncommon for differences in cultural values, norms, and patterns to become frustrating to the point of being overwhelming. This is often accompanied by the realization that *"These people actually live life this way!"* That realization is accompanied by the twin awareness that *"If they live life like this, they must not live the way* we *do."* It is almost as though we thought they were kind of kidding, and that really we all have the same need to be efficient (or relational, or whichever cultural value is in view) that my people do.

By the way, this can also happen for people visiting you! For example, short-term visitors to the US are often very appreciative of our efficiency, innovation, and egalitarian access to the markets. Yet after several months here, they may begin to long for the hierarchies, stability, and structure that we eschew in favor of being able to move quickly, or whatever the norms are from their particular place of origin.

This second stage, which begins with **disenchantment**, almost always deteriorates further. Initially, this might look like a kind of growing **apathy** or **ambivalence** regarding the host culture. However, this feeling may (and often does) sink into a passionate dislike or even hatred for the host culture. There are several factors at work here that cause this emotionally heightened response.

A. The sojourner experiences normal homesickness that accompanies being away from one's own place and people for an extended period of time (apparent even within very similar cultures—for example, a Nebraskan visiting relatives in Kansas will often experience homesickness after a couple of months).

B. The demands of the sojourn normally pick up after the first couple of months. There is often a real or imagined grace period at the beginning of an international move to allow for the transition. However, after a few months, you will be expected to function at high capacity. Neither hosts nor sponsors back home (like bosses or teachers) usually expect you to have difficulty after the initial adjustment—especially if you sent back rosy reports during the emotionally high stage.

C. By this point in the sojourn, many of the deeper cultural differences have begun to be really apparent. However, there has not been enough time to develop and hone skills for this culture. Thus, the distance between what you need to be learning and your actual level of functionality becomes apparent, which can be especially discouraging. Moreover, by this point, sojourners have usually started to uncover some deeply troubling realities about the host culture that they have not yet been able to process.

D. The increasing sense of role deprivation means that the normal ways in which you would reassure yourself that you are a competent and valuable member of a team (or society) are no longer available to you. This deepens the disruptiveness of the issues already mentioned.

This stage is not a straightforward downward slope, as there will be some (often small) successes along the way. However, sometimes these successes give rise to even greater disappointment. This is especially true for language learning.[20] Increasing your ability to conjugate verbs, for example, may result in the realization that there is a whole tense that you have not been using, or perhaps worse, have developed patterns of misusing.

I have included the word *depression* in the title of this subsection, and it is important to clarify what I mean here. *First*, recalling that culture shock is cumulative, the combined effects of continued disappointment, sadness (as in missing home), and frustration can lead to emotional, mental, and physical fatigue. In concert, these symptoms can present in a way that appears very similar to clinical depression. When I have known people who decided to stop taking anti-depressants during transitions, it has seemed to not go well for them. Sometimes people view a cross-cultural transition as a time to reinvent themselves, but it's really important to thoroughly consult with a mental health or medical professional before making a regimen change like that.

Second, although culture shock often looks like depression, I have known quite a few people who are able to exit it without the assistance of (new) medications or counseling. Although culture shock is cumulative, it is also transitory, meaning that it almost always passes with time. No blanket statement can cover all of the possible ways this could play out, so it is important to be forthright with your mental health provider if you are experiencing these kinds of disruptions.[21]

What's more, if the depressive symptoms of culture shock are hanging around without any noticeable improvement, it may be a good idea to seek professional mental health support, as unresolving culture shock may be related to adjustment disorder.[22] The next two chapters will more fully address the typical symptoms of culture shock. For now, we will turn to the more encouraging news about culture shock—the way out!

3) CONFIDENCE AND COMPETENCE

After a period of what can feel like a free fall toward personal and professional **disintegration**, sojourners will begin to realize that they have started to stabilize. A new normal arises, with patterns of living that become more predictable and productive. This is not something that you can force to happen on your own timeline, but for nearly everyone who goes through culture shock, there is a moment when you realize that things are not as bad as they were before. Slowly but surely, you begin to develop specific competencies related to your responsibilities. At the same time, you begin to develop social skills that are appropriate for the context. Finally, you also begin to develop realistic expectations about communication with friends, families, and the workplace both in your new location and back home.

This stage usually involves a relatively long process of trial and error, and it usually includes one or more major setbacks. However, the general trajectory is back toward emotional stability and efficacy. As you grow into the new culture, you may begin the real process of adapting to the culture. This is to some degree dependent on your level of **intercultural competence**.[23] Regardless of your level of intercultural competence, this is a stage of increasing confidence and usually signals the slow, but real, end of culture shock—unless and until you return home. Chapter 6 deals with the process of returning home and the struggles that often accompany this transition.

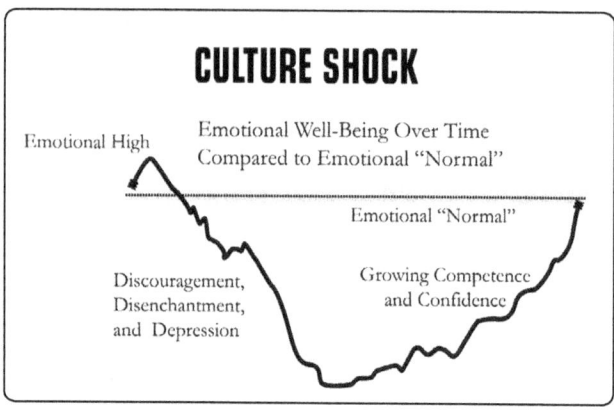

For more information visit: https://cultureshock.traxcultures.com

CONCEPT 12

Train yourself to recognize the symptoms of culture shock

I am often surprised at how people who are right in the midst of culture shock fail to recognize their situation. While they may admit they are experiencing discomfort, they often assume that the issue is something else, and they are at times even hostile to the idea that they are experiencing culture shock. I think that sometimes people view it as a kind of failure, which it is not. In fact, I tend more to think it is evidence that you are actually engaging with the experience, and it is thus a good (albeit very uncomfortable) sign.

I am including a list of symptoms that my students have found very helpful. I recommend reading through this list at least once every couple of weeks while in the midst of a cross-cultural transition, to see whether you are experiencing culture shock. These ideas have been adapted and expanded from L. Robert Kohls' very useful book called *Survival Kit for Overseas Living*.[24] (I recommend picking up a copy.) Please note that any of these symptoms, or any combination of them, may also be a sign of another physical or mental health issue unrelated to culture shock, so be sure to consult your care provider.

▷ feeling an unusual amount of anxiety or boredom that is not easily resolved,

▷ experiencing homesickness—sometimes significantly so, and often in unexpected ways,

▷ an exaggerated feeling of being helpless or inadequate,

▷ experience emotions that you would categorize as sad or depressive (see the discussion of depression on the previous pages),

▷ drowsiness and/or fatigue that doesn't resolve even with a good amount of sleep,

▷ an exaggerated inability to make decisions,

- persistent, unwelcome, and sometimes disabling self-doubt,
- unexplained emotions and emotional outbursts like anger, weeping, or laughter,
- succumbing to (or harboring) an irrational belief that others are intentionally sabotaging you,
- physical (psychosomatic) illnesses, persistent colds, difficulties with digestion,
- physically hiding away from others, such as by spending excessive amounts of time in your hotel room, apartment, or dorm room,
- being physically present but mentally withdrawing, such as by daydreaming,
- spending large amounts of time reading or watching TV or movies, especially if it is more time than what you would normally do at home,
- spending excessive amounts of time sleeping,
- interacting only with people who are culturally like you, or, in some cases, only with people who are culturally different from you,

- having an inability to pay attention to others or to tasks for a long period of time,

- losing the ability to study or work effectively, or to think clearly,

- eating excessively or compulsively (comfort eating),

- drinking mood-altering drinks like coffee or alcohol excessively or compulsively,

- developing a new or exaggerated need for cleanliness, or an unusually heightened awareness of uncleanliness,

- irritability, irrational anger, emotional outbursts,

- tension with coworkers, teammates, peers, or family,

- the exaggeration of controlling tendencies—even if these are for the "benefit" of others,

- an increased reliance on simplified **frames for understanding** differences—such as using stereotypes to understand your own or the host culture. This can also be applied to gender,

- ▷ Latent or expressive hostility toward members of the host culture or of your own culture,

- ▷ unusual levels of verbal, physical, or sexual aggressiveness. Physical aggressiveness can include road rage as well as other kinds of hostility,

- ▷ experiencing lapses in clarity regarding ethical reasoning,

- ▷ the unwelcome presence and persistence of doubt as regards your faith background.

It may surprise you to learn that the majority of my students have experienced at least two-thirds of these symptoms at some point during their cross-cultural transitions. It is important to understand that these are symptoms of culture shock for two reasons. First, imagine that you have recently arrived in another country and find yourself exhibiting these symptoms but don't realize that they are being caused by culture shock. I have seen people in this state—they begin to assume that the symptoms are actually problems with themselves. ("I don't even recognize myself! I'm not this kind of a person!") Thus, understanding these symptoms helps people to have more grace for themselves and their companions through the culture shock process. Second, recognizing culture shock at work in yourself can alert you to the reality that you may be attempting to cope with the stress in a way that is ultimately unhealthy. This idea is addressed more fully in Concept 17.

It is important to remember that this book is intended as a general guide and will not be appropriate for all situations. I especially recommend *The Psychology of Culture Shock* (second edition) by Ward, Bochner, and Furnham for a more in-depth discussion of culture shock.[25] The content in my book is in no way intended to replace competent medical or psychological assistance, and readers are urged to consult with these professionals as appropriate.

NOTES

[15] Originally introduced by: Oberg, K. (1960). Cultural Shock: Adjustment to New Cultural Environments. Practical Anthropology, os-7(4), 177–182. https://doi.org/10.1177/009182966000700405

[16] See also Fitzpatrick, F. (2017). Taking the "culture" out of "culture shock"—a critical review of literature on cross-cultural adjustment in international relocation. Critical Perspectives on International Business, 13(4), 278–296. https://doi.org/10.1108/cpoib-01-2017-0008

[17] Furnham, A. (2019). Culture Shock: A Review of the Literature for Practitioners. *Psychology*, *10*, 1832. §2 https://doi.org/10.4236/psych.2019.1013119

[18] Furnham, A. (2019). Culture Shock: A Review of the Literature for Practitioners. *Psychology*, *10*, 1832. §2 https://doi.org/10.4236/psych.2019.1013119

[19] The use of the word *depression* is complicated: it is not intended to be denotative of the mental health diagnosis. Instead, it is intended in a colloquial sense, as when a person says "I feel so depressed." For a discussion of depression in culture shock, see Furnham, A. (2019). Culture Shock: A Review of the Literature for Practitioners. Psychology, 10, 1832. https://doi.org/10.4236/psych.2019.1013119

[20] Paige, R. M., Cohen, A. D., Kappler, B., Chi, J. C., & Lassegard, J. P. (2006). Maximizing Study Abroad a Student's Guide to Strategies for Language and Culture Learning and Use (2nd ed.). Board of Regents University of Minnesota. For more visit: https://maxsa.traxcultures.com

[21] This book should not be interpreted as containing professional mental health advice. See your mental health and/or medical provider for professional advice.

[22] Lucas, J. (2009). Over-stressed, Overwhelmed, and Over Here: Resident Directors and the Challenges of Student Mental Health Abroad. *Frontiers: The Interdisciplinary Journal of Study Abroad*, XVIII, 187–216.

[23] Find much more about intercultural competence at https://iccompetence.traxcultures.com

[24] Kohls, Robert L. (2001). *Survival kit for overseas living: For Americans planning to live and work abroad.* (4th Ed.). Boston, MA: Nicholas Brealey. For more visit: https://survivalkit.traxcultures.com

[25] Ward, C., Bochner, S., & Furnham, A. (2001). *The Psychology of Culture Shock* (2nd ed.). Routledge. More at: https://psyofcs.traxcultures.com/

CHAPTER FIVE

PREPARING FOR CROSS-CULTURAL SUCCESS

One of the things that has long baffled me about my college students comes up when I ask them about their expectations for their upcoming trip. Many of them say, "Well, I don't really have any." If I seem surprised, they say, "I'm trying to keep an open mind so I get the most out of the trip." Although this is a nice sentiment, it is simply not true that they have no expectations.

CONCEPT 13

Acknowledge your expectations

Everyone who engages in cross-cultural transitions has **expectations**. Businesspeople are often at least more straightforward about their expectations than students tend to be. The better you do at acknowledging your expectations, the better you will do processing the cross-cultural transition. Here's why: *many of your expectations will be* *frustrated*. If you acknowledge that certain goals are important to you, then you can recognize that they are not being met and respond to this as it happens. Otherwise, you will just be left with a vague sense of unease and likely misattribute the cause to a relatively innocent source.

Consider this story of our unfortunate traveler, James:

••

James is a sales rep for a US manufacturer looking to do business overseas. Before leaving on his month-long sales trip, his wife asks what his expectations are for the journey. He tells her, "I'm planning to make at least one big sale in each country I visit." She is supportive of his goals, and he sets off with this plan in mind.

In the first country James visits, he meets his contact and begins discussing business on the way from the airport to the office. He doesn't get this sale and adjusts his tack with the next contact, waiting until his host brings up the business deal. Although he gets this sale, it isn't as big as he hoped for. With the third, fourth, and fifth businesses he interacts with, he is able to make a big sale, but he consistently feels like there is something he is missing in the interactions with the hosts.

In the meantime, James is frustrated that his cell phone and credit card only work some of the time. After a week on the road, he gives up on trying to talk with his wife every day. After two weeks of travel, their conversations have grown increasingly short and tense, and he is frustrated that she can't understand what he's talking about.

By the fourth week, James is ready to come home. Even though he has met his sales goal, he is sick of being on the road and is disappointed with the overall experience of traveling. The people he has been interacting with are friendly, but he doesn't really feel like he can trust them. At the same time, he's not sure how things will be with his wife, since they weren't able to talk for the last week because the internet was too slow for Facetime, and his phone wasn't working anymore anyway.

••••••••••••••••••••••••••••••••••••••

This brief story is intended to illustrate that James actually had a lot of expectations he didn't state before leaving. The sales goal was a stated expectation, but in spite of meeting it, he had an overall negative experience. Here are a few of his unstated expectations:

▷ James expected to be received as a competent professional. When his normal approaches to sales didn't work, he adjusted, but it was frustrating to him that he came across as incompetent.

▷ James expected to be able to develop rapport, and even a professional friendship, with some of his contacts. He expected to be able to do this in a way that was familiar to him, according to patterns that he considered "normal."

▷ James expected to be able to maintain good relations with his wife while traveling. He specifically expected to be able to talk with her at least four times a week. He also expected his wife to be able to understand what he was experiencing.

▷ James expected his technological and financial tools to work without fail.

▷ James expected his return to be a happy one, without marital tension.

▷ James expected that he would really enjoy the trip and that this would be the first of many trips like it.

None of these expectations was unreasonable. However, it was unlikely that any or all of them would be fulfilled in the way James expected. Of course, simply listing these expectations would not cause them to happen.

What creating a comprehensive and authentic assessment of expectations *does* accomplish, however, is to make it possible to compare the actual experience to the expected experience. This in turn illuminates what might be causing frustrations and tensions during the sojourn. The best practice is to create an honest list of expectations before traveling, and to revisit it from time to time to see what did and did not come to fruition. Naturally, it may also be necessary to add to the list as new, formerly hidden, expectations come to light.

CONCEPT 14

Don't just be yourself

One of the more ill-conceived recommendations I have heard for a cross-cultural sojourner is this: "When you're over there, just be yourself!" Again, although the sentiment is a nice one, it is inappropriate for cross-cultural transitions. We define ourselves and our patterns in relation to our own culture, and when we import this cultural self into a host culture, there are elements that simply don't fit.

Think of it this way: within our own culture, we recognize that different behaviors are appropriate in different circumstances. The exuberance expressed at a football game is generally inappropriate for the workplace and vice versa. Yet both ranges of expression (football and workplace) may be part of who you are. The difference is that in the intercultural setting, we often do not yet have the appropriate range of expression.

Thus, whether you use your business self, your church self, or your party animal self, none of these personas are tuned to the demands of the cross-cultural setting. It is not appropriate to just be yourself, any more than it is appropriate to act in a court of law as though it were a sports bar simply because you are your more accurate self when in a bar. Instead, you have to adapt and expand what it means to be you when in a cross-cultural setting, just as you would when in an unfamiliar setting at home.

That said, it is important to recognize that there are certain elements of who you are that remain constant. If you are a husband or wife, or mother or father embarking on a trip, this does not change just because you are in a different culture. Travel is not license to disregard or lose sight of the permanent elements of who you are; however, they might have to be expressed differently in the culture you are visiting.

CONCEPT 15

Learn to recognize the factors that intensify the experience

It is very common for people to have difficulty comprehending why it is that cross-cultural transitions can be so disruptive. Although we have already covered a number of those topics, this section presents another way to think about the disruption present in cross-cultural transition, using the idea of **intensity factors**. R. Michael Paige, one of the foremost international educators of his day, created a comprehensive list to explain what it is that makes intercultural experiences so intense.[26] I have adapted and expanded on his ideas here.

▷ The more *cultural difference* that exists between the sojourner's host and home cultures, the more difficult the experience will be. In thinking about this idea, it is important to remember that cultures contain so many factors that it might be easy to underestimate the actual amount of difference. What's more, if you tend to view the differences as overly positive or negative, it can make the differences even more difficult to process, and thus more intense.

▷ In general, the less *interculturally competent* a person is, the more intense the experience will be.[27] **Intercultural competence** can be seen as a spectrum moving between **monocultural** (my culture is the only way) at one end and **global** (I understand my culture relative to other cultures) at the other. At the global end of the spectrum, people begin to develop the skill of **frame shifting** for the way they think and act so they can move between cultures more naturally. The more people see their own culture as central to reality, the more intense the experience will probably be for them. Prejudice increases the experience of intensity.[28]

▷ Language plays a complicated role in increasing intensity in the cross-cultural sojourn. On the one hand, a lack of fluency in the host language causes a significant increase in intensity because language is so important, not only in communicating ideas but also in the way that logic works. On the other hand, at times the use of a good interpreter (who can translate not only words but ideas) actually serves as a buffer against the real differences present between cultures, thus lowering the intensity of the experience. In this way, linguistic competence may actually increase intensity. It is, after all, very disturbing to hear someone say something you understand linguistically but not logically or experientially. Nonetheless, increased **linguistic competence** in general will lower the intensity of an experience.

▷ The degree to which you experience *immersion* in the host culture also affects the cross-cultural intensity of the experience. If you tend to remain with other people from your own country and are able to stay at familiar hotels or lodging and eat at familiar-seeming restaurants, the experience will be less intense overall. However, these choices may at the same time create a significant barrier between you and your hosts, depending on the nature of your business. With some of the work I was involved with, we did not start making relational progress until we stayed in the homes of our hosts. This is of course more intense, but it was the most appropriate solution in that situation.

▷ In general, possessing *previous intercultural experience* helps reduce the intensity of cross-cultural transitions. There are two caveats to this. First, it is possible to be present in a location without actually being present to the culture. This could happen, for example, when an American is having an American experience even when in a Japanese location. In such a case, the experience might not actually be intercultural, and if so it would then not be likely to reduce the intensity of the next experience. The second caveat flows from the first in that sometimes people assume they are better at crossing cultures than they actually are. For a person like this, like the student of mine I mentioned in the second chapter, a hard bout of culture shock can be deeply unsettling.

▷ One of the more complicated intensity factors relates to relative visibility. If a person is used to being a visible member of the majority group in their home culture (for example, being white in America), it can be difficult to suddenly be a visible minority (such as being white in sub-Sarahan Africa). On the other hand, a person who is used to being a visible minority (such as being black in America) may find it unsettling how their minority / majority experience is interpreted in the host culture. This happened to African American poet Langston Hughes, who was interpreted as being white while visiting Africa a century ago.[29] He recounted having been deeply hurt by the fact that people did not perceive him to be Black.[30]

This provided significant fodder for reflection for Hughes, who used the disconnect between his own self-perception and others' perception to better understand his identity. It is important to be aware that your own ethnic identity might be either unknown or misinterpreted while you are out of your home culture.

▷ Cross-cultural transitions can also bring about a change in *perceived or relative status*. For my students who visited developing countries, this took the form of reinterpreting themselves not as poor college students but as relatively wealthy foreigners (though of course this depends on who they were interacting with). That was a very unsettling transition for many of them. On the other hand, you may find that your particular credential may not be recognized, thus lowering your status when visiting another country. For example, not everyone who is called "doctor" in their country could retain the title while in Germany, depending on what kind of degree has earned them that title.[31]

▷ One of the most frustrating intensity factors can be related to *power and control*. For example, for Americans, who are often used to a high degree of **agency** (taking care of and making decisions for themselves), it can be unnerving to play the role of guest. To be subject to the bureaucracy, or even the hospitality, of another culture can be significantly frustrating for many Americans.

▷ I have also found that *team relationships*, when a factor, can definitely increase the experience of intensity in the cross-cultural setting. Teams can be a great source of comfort and encouragement, but even normally functional teams can quickly disintegrate under the stress generated by culture shock.

- *Romance between* the sojourner and anyone else is another intensity factor. Whether with a committed significant other at home, a team-member, a spouse traveling with you, or a member of the host culture, romantic relationships can increase the intensity of the sojourn. This is not to say that they need to be entirely avoided, but rather it should be understood that they are not neutral factors.

- *The living environment* is the final intensity factor. This can take several forms, including climate, access to palatable food and beverage, access to medical care, and the presence of various threats like stinging or biting insects or animals, venomous or irritant plants, and the presence and severity of unfamiliar diseases. I have seen situations where sojourners were so focused on the living environment that they were unable to engage the culture meaningfully. Adequate preparation in this respect (without creating paranoia) is very important for most sojourners traveling to places with difficult living situations.

CONCEPT 16

Be aware of the factors that increase risk

In addition to the factors that increase intensity of cross-cultural sojourns, there are also a number of factors that can increase the experience of risk. These factors also make the experience potentially more difficult, and it is wise to be familiar with them so as to adequately prepare for and understand the experience. I recommend conducting a regular (every two weeks or so) review of both the intensity factors and the risk factors to reflect on how they may be impacting your experience. This list is again adapted and expanded from R. Michael Paige's original conceptualization of the **risk factors**.[32]

▷ Different cultures have different *public and private boundaries*, so elements of your life that ordinarily remain private (particularly in business settings) may be brought out into the open or probed while on a sojourn. This may cause incredible discomfort. On the other hand, areas of your personal life that you want others to know might not be interesting or appropriate from the perspective of your hosts.

- Due to the difficulty in cross-cultural transitions, there is a fairly high *risk of failure* to meet expectations. Depending on your (and your organization's) threshold for failure, this possibility may be more or less acceptable. If possible, it is best to plan for a certain amount of failure and to create contingency plans to accommodate this. Failure can be particularly threatening to people with personality types that strive to be seen as successful and to be affirmed all around.

- *Embarrassment and offense* are certainties while in cross-cultural transition. You will be embarrassed and offended and you will embarrass and offend others. Plan for this, and do not be surprised when it happens. It can be difficult to know how to plan for contingencies, but it is a good idea to study how to make proper apologies in the culture in which you are a guest. This information will also help you recognize apologies if and when they come your way.

- Depending on how interculturally competent you are at the beginning of your sojourn, and what kind of identity work you have already accomplished, you may find different kinds of threats to your *cultural identity*. In some cases, you may find that people reject certain elements of your culture that are very important to you. In other cases, you may find yourself rejecting your own culture. If you begin to identify with the host culture, you may also find yourself dealing with difficult issues about what culture you actually belong to. This issue is not limited to people on long-term transitions abroad. Even people on very short trips may find that their sense of being alienated from their own culture is somehow inflamed by the travel.

▷ One of the most threatening risks that I have observed is that of *self-awareness*. On the one hand, **self-awareness** is an incredibly important skill for successful cross-cultural transitions. On the other hand, new awareness about oneself can be absolutely crippling in the short run. The risk of finding out how good you aren't at things you care about, for example, can be tremendously discouraging.

▷ *Role deprivation* can provide a significant amount of risks to a person's self-perception. There are many different ways this plays out, but essentially the new cultural setting does not (at least at first) allow you to express the roles you are used to. For example, some professional roles may not be available to you depending on whether your credentials are accepted. However, even if you will fill a role very similar to your previous occupation, months or years of language and culture study may sideline you in the short run. Additionally, lack of social roles such as those enjoyed in clubs, religious organizations, and similar groups may further a sense of role deprivation. Moreover, certain practical and legal restrictions may change the way your family operates, which can lead to further disruption or deprivation of your role.

In my experience working with students abroad, the two most intense factors from this list and the previous list are *team relations* and *self-awareness*, with *living environment* a close third in some cases.

CONCEPT 17

Prepare yourself to cope and be vigilant

In light of everything up to this point in this chapter, you might feel a little discouraged. The truth is that cross-cultural transitions are difficult, and their effect should not be underestimated. There is one more thing that we need to cover, and it is really important to your success in navigating (or helping someone else navigate) cross-cultural transitions: **coping.**

Given the psychological, emotional, and physical stresses mentioned in this chapter, you undoubtedly need ways to cope with the stress. The reality is that *you will cope*. The question is *how*. I urge you to develop a coping plan before or early in the trip or move, and to revisit it regularly. Healthy coping is important for your ability to continue to engage the culture and to accomplish the goals you set out to complete. Moreover, healthy coping is an important skill for finding access to long-term, high-quality, healthy friendships.

On the other hand, I feel compelled to issue a very stark warning: Unhealthy coping can absolutely undo you. Everyone has vices he or she is prone to. For some these are sexual; for some they are substance-related; for some they are financial, such as with gambling; for some they are relational or involve manipulation of or power over others; and for others these involve self-deprivation or self-harm. There are, of course, many other vices, but you should not deceive yourself into imagining that you do not have your go-to vices. The reason these may not be readily apparent to you is that most of us have created networks and points of contact in our normal lives that reaffirm the better parts of who we are and keep the worse parts of who we are in check.

In the cross-cultural transition, most of our sources of positive affirmation and moral guidance are suddenly absent. Not only that, but we find ourselves in a new cultural milieu with its own moral realities and complications. In such a setting, particularly when under stress, it can be easy to lose our moral bearings much more quickly than you might imagine possible. I remember one time, on the same day I was presenting this section while doing a training for an organization, the leaders were notified of a significant personnel issue that resulted from unhealthy coping. The consequences of unhealthy coping are significant, costly, and affect many people—not just you.

For this reason, I highly recommend two action points. *First*, create a plan for how you can cope healthily. For example, allow yourself a certain amount of the comforts of home if they are available— movies, books, magazines, food, music—that keep you tied into home and comfort. Find creative outlets for stress, such as exercise, cooking, writing, or painting. You don't have to be particularly good at any of these things for them to help you.

There are situations in which your normal coping mechanisms (running, for example) may not be available to you for cultural or safety reasons. Plan ahead on alternatives so that you are empowered to continue coping in a healthy way rather than being overwhelmed by this setback. It is a great idea to find a mentor or coach who understands cross-cultural transitions who can help you process things when they get too deep. Very often newcomers to an international environment are disappointed by the lack of mentoring and support they encounter when they arrive. It is often a good idea to exercise agency and find someone in advance who can support and mentor you even if it means connecting from time to time over the internet.

The *second* action point is to regularly review the symptoms of culture shock listed in the previous chapter. When you start to recognize that you are exhibiting these symptoms, give yourself plenty of grace. At the same time, create healthy limits that will keep you from the worst outcomes of those symptoms. Also, watch for ways these might be playing out that you didn't expect. Physical aggressiveness, for example, may manifest in driving like an idiot rather than in punching someone. If you sense that you are getting in too deep, call a mentor.

One thing to be especially careful of is emotional dependency. There is a tendency present in many people, which can at times cross over into an actual psychological disorder (talk to your mental health provider), to overly attach yourself to another person, particularly in a time of intense stress. This feeling will often masquerade as love, but it tends to be very self-serving and often has characteristics of intense jealousy and possessiveness. This tendency can be absolutely destructive, especially (but not only) in the event it is at cross-purposes with the goal of your sojourn. Both in the emotional and sexual realms, this method of coping can have real and lasting consequences. A good mentor or psychologist can help you recognize and avoid these kinds of relationships and find alternative, healthier ways to cope.

CONCEPT 18

Engage in constructive preparation

There are several good ways to ready yourself for a cultural transition. Of course, one of the most important mechanisms for this is preparing yourself through increased self-awareness. Self-awareness that happens prior to the sojourn is usually not as threatening as self-awareness that is generated by the sojourn.

Another helpful kind of preparation is what I call *constructive preparation*. This kind of preparation involves becoming increasingly familiar with the culture you will be transitioning to prior to your departure. Here are a few ideas on how to do that:

- ▷ Watch movies and documentaries that take place in the culture you are visiting. You can also include the experiences of people from the place you are visiting while they themselves are abroad. If you are going to France, you could watch movies that take place in France as well as movies about French people in America.

- ▷ Read travel guides, travelogues, and blogs from people who have gone before you. For culture-specific information, I especially recommend the Culture Shock series and anything published by Intercultural Press.[33]

- ▷ Take a class on the culture of the place you'll be going to.

- ▷ Check out books from the library. I especially recommend books with lots of pictures, as they help you imagine where you are going.

- ▷ If there is a mechanism to do this, try to meet people from the host culture before you go. For example, sometimes you can volunteer to help international students at local colleges and universities.

- ▷ Learn about the history of your host culture. Politics, religion, and economics are really useful in providing context.

- ▷ Find an expat website specific to the location you are moving to.

As always, this list comes with a series of caveats. First, any media representation of the place you are going will be incomplete and often biased. That's okay as long as you recognize the limitation. Second, if you are able to make friends before you go, be aware that there may be expectations placed on you because of that relationship. For example, in some cultures friendship connections carry with them the expectation of financial assistance for the friend and his family. Importantly, this does not always negate the validity of the friendship, as it may instead be a sign of the friendship. Nonetheless, being a friend may come with strings attached, and it is good to be aware upfront that this is possible.

CONCEPT 19

Make friends

Once you arrive, one of the things that will serve you well is to make friends in the host culture. A good host-culture friend will be able to serve as a guide and help you understand things you aren't attuned to. A good host-culture friend will also be able to point out *faux pas* that you may be committing without realizing it.

If you don't already have a group of people around you from your own culture, it's also a good idea to make friends with a few expats, if they are available. People from your own country can give you pointers on how to navigate the local **bureaucracy**, the best places to eat, and what to avoid. They can also serve as a good outlet for commiserating about shared frustrations with the host culture.

Again, there are a couple of caveats in order here. First, when making friends across cultures, recognize that the people most likely to engage in relationship with you are often themselves somewhat marginal in their own culture. People who are within the "normal" range of their own culture are often not particularly incentivized to reach out to foreigners. Those who do reach out to you may be doing so because you represent a way of thinking they find attractive, or because you are in some way exotic to them. This does not mean that you need to avoid these friendships, but it does mean that they can limit your ability to connect with non-marginal groups, so they must be handled carefully. If your role is particularly strategic, it is probably worth pushing past the "low hanging" relational fruit and investing the hard work in developing relationships with more culturally central people.

A second thing about making friends with cultural hosts is that in some cultures, this will mean making friends with the whole family. You'll need to check the cultural norms in your area, but it would not be uncommon for you to be invited into family situations that would seem odd to bring a stranger into in your own culture. Again, not a big problem, but something to be aware of.

Third, friendship norms vary widely by culture. One the one hand, you might perceive more friendship than actually exists. For example, if you are sojourning to a place where people are generally relationally "warmer" than they are in your culture, you might misread this as a stronger affirmation than exists. On the other hand, you yourself might overrepresent your level of friendship with someone. In some cultures, the very word *friend* (or its translation) comes with specific responsibilities, and a failure to live up to these may reveal you to be a "false friend" even if you never knew the responsibilities existed.

Finally, on expats, there are a couple of considerations. Beware the jaded expat. There are some who have such a negative attitude about the host culture (or their own culture!) that it will be difficult for you to avoid being affected by this. Less damaging is the hopelessly optimistic expat, who refuses to take an honest look at the problems in the host culture, when of course such problems do exist. Also beware that affiliations with various people from your own culture can influence how your hosts interpret you. I have seen people unintentionally discredit themselves by keeping company with co-nationals that had bad reputations in the host community.

CONCEPT 20

Have fun

This chapter has covered some of the more difficult realities that you should prepare for in the cross-cultural transition. While many of these concepts have a negative tone, crossing cultures can be one of the most rewarding and exciting human endeavors.

One of the best ways to have a successful cross-cultural experience is to have fun. Explore. Meet people. Ask questions. Be surprised. Be amazed. Record your sense of wonder. Collaborate. Embrace the experience. Enjoy the adventure. Innovate. This is really important! Be an agent of your own cross-cultural transition. Practice gratitude and celebration.

Cross-cultural transitions open your eyes to possibilities that you never could have seen otherwise—for yourself, for your business or cause, and for humanity. Engage the possibilities.

NOTES

[26] Paige, R. Michael. (1993). "On the nature of intercultural experiences and intercultural education." *Education for the intercultural experience.* (2nd Ed.). Edited by R. Michael Paige. Yarmouth, ME: Intercultural Press. More at: https://edforic.traxcultures.com

[27] See also Presbitero, A. (2016). Culture shock and reverse culture shock: The moderating role of cultural intelligence in international students' adaptation. International Journal of Intercultural Relations, 53, 28–38. https://doi.org/10.1016/j.ijintrel.2016.05.004

[28] Goldstein, S. B., & Keller, S. R. (2015). U.S. college students' lay theories of culture shock. International Journal of Intercultural Relations, 47, 187–194. https://doi.org/10.1016/j.ijintrel.2015.05.010

[29] Hughes, L. (1993). The Big Sea: An Autobiography (2nd Hill and Wang ed). New York: Hill and Wang. p. 103 https://thebigsea.traxcultures.com

[30] Hughes, L. (1993). The Big Sea: An Autobiography (2nd Hill and Wang ed). New York: Hill and Wang. p. 11 https://thebigsea.traxcultures.com

[31] Central Office for Foreign Education. (n.d.). Retrieved December 8, 2019, from https://www.kmk.org/zab/central-office-for-foreign-education.html

[32] Paige, R. Michael. (1993). "On the nature of intercultural experiences and intercultural education." *Education for the intercultural experience*. (2nd Ed.). Edited by R. Michael Paige. Yarmouth, ME: Intercultural Press. More at: https://edforic.traxcultures.com

[33] See https://icpress.traxcultures.com for a list of recommendations.

CHAPTER SIX

COMING HOME AND WELCOMING BACK

This chapter of *Transitions Across Cultures* will help you prepare for the process of coming home after a cross-cultural sojourn. It is also intended to help you welcome back a friend or loved one who has been traveling.

CONCEPT 21

Coming home is transition all over again

For sojourners who have been gone for more than a couple of weeks (the exact amount of time will vary), the transition home follows essentially the same pattern as the transition abroad. There is a new set of endings, another neutral zone, and a new set of beginnings. The thread of continuity will again have to be rediscovered.

CONCEPT 22

Home just kind of . . . isn't

On returning home, culture shock will often play out again, although in this case, it is called **reentry shock**. Somewhat surprisingly, reentry shock is caused by basically the same tensions and realities that caused culture shock to begin with. The mental map of how the world works has to flex back to fit the home culture. However, depending on how long you have been gone, the home culture has likely changed since you left.

This is actually one of the most disturbing things about reentry shock. During a period of culture shock, many people (refugees and asylees excluded) have the reserve option to check out and return home. "No matter how bad it is here," you might reason, "I could go home, and everything would be back to normal." The problem with this idea is twofold. *First*, as the sojourner, you may be indelibly changed by even a short experience. Thus, you are not the same "you" who left to embark on the sojourn. *Second*, home has changed. Your own culture has moved on in your absence, generating, experiencing, and processing realities that you might not have, including tragedies, elections, and triumphs. This is true of family and friends, too. You have likely missed out on graduations, weddings, births, divorces, and deaths. Your family and friends have already finished processing information you might just be finding out about.

The cumulative effect is that on returning home, it almost always doesn't feel quite like home. This can be far more disruptive than the initial culture shock. Because if home doesn't feel like home . . . what does?

CONCEPT 23

Do the transition well

Transitioning home can be done both well and poorly. Here are a few pointers for transitioning home well. *Before you leave the host culture*:

▷ Process the new set of endings. What will no longer be true about you once you leave?

▷ To the extent as it is possible, reconcile any difficult relationships in the host culture. It is infinitely harder to accomplish this after leaving.

▷ Make a list of what you have experienced that really matters to you—you'll want to come back to this later.

> Write down the insights that the time in the host culture has given you. These might seem crystal clear at the moment, but they will get unexpectedly fuzzy after you leave.

> Make a list of what you want to do if you ever come back to the host culture. Don't assume that you inevitably will return. All sorts of things can keep this from happening.

> It's not a bad idea to get pictures of friends, phone numbers, emails addresses, and social media contacts.

> Do not make promises you can't keep. It is often tempting to say, "I'll be back next year," or "I'll call you once a week." These might even seem reasonable at the moment, but they are generally unreasonable expectations. If you value the relationships you've developed, don't make unrealistic promises. This applies both to hosts and teammates.

Upon leaving the host culture, inasmuch as it is up to you, DO NOT GO STRAIGHT HOME. For a trip of roughly six weeks or longer, I recommend a minimum of three to five full days in a third culture—a neutral location for a debrief. This is more important than most travelers realize, and for some it can be hard to justify the cost. However, from my perspective this is absolutely one of the most important pieces of advice about the return home.

When you are still in your host culture, there are some things that you will not be able to process because they are too close at hand. Not only that, but it can be hard to believe that you are really leaving, which can make processing nearly impossible. As soon as you arrive home, there are expectations (both your own and others') that make it difficult to process the immediate transition. Moreover, once you are home, it is too late to prepare to go home! So what to do while in the third location?

▷ Rest and relaxation. This is a serious recommendation and is not in the least bit frivolous. Returning home rested will greatly improve the first week of transition.

▷ Map out what has happened during your sojourn. I recommend making a month-by-month map of your social, cultural, academic, economic, and spiritual well-being from their sojourn. Each topic gets its own color, and these maps are drawn using the landscape orientation on a piece of paper. Significant moments of change are marked with words of explanation.

102 | TRANSITIONS ACROSS CULTURES

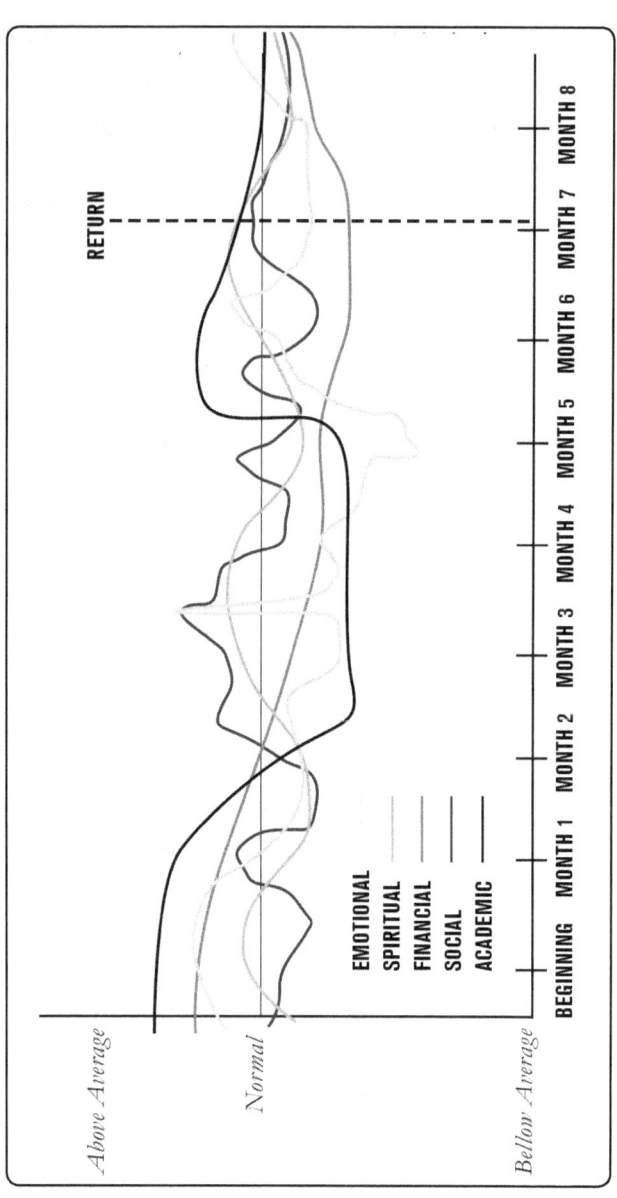

▷ Look through the headlines of news and movies that came out back home in the last several months, so you have some sense of what people are talking about upon your return.

▷ Create an **elevator speech** in which you can describe your experience in 30 seconds or less. Although many people will express interest, few (at least in American culture) are interested in hearing more than about a minute of your experience. Creating a couple of concise explanations of your experience will allow you to share something of meaning in a way that lets you play it safe.

•••••••••••••••••••••••••••••••••••••••

SAMPLE ELEVATOR SPEECH

Friend: *How was your trip? I want to hear all about it!*

Response: *I really learned a lot! I was gone for six months and was able to spend time in Africa and France. I was surprised by how good and how hard it was, but I made some great friends. One of the most surprising things I learned was all of the different ways that people can see the world!*

Friend: *Sounds fascinating! I'd love to see pictures sometime. Gotta run—see you later!*

●●●●●●●●●●●●●●●●●●●●●●●●●●●●●●●●●●●●●●●

▷ Prepare yourself for disappointment. The reality is that many of your friends and family will not understand what a life-changing, challenging, or wonderful sojourn you have been on. Even more disappointing, depending on how long you have been gone, there may actually be people who ask you when you are going to leave on the trip—even if you've been out of the country for six months or more!

▷ Develop a list of expectations for your return home. Just like the trip abroad, the more honest you are about the expectations you have for going home, the better you will be able to process what happens. Many people have "scripts" that play in their heads about what it will be like to be welcomed home.

I remember a student who had imagined her parents waiting expectantly by the baggage claim, holding signs and thrilled to see her. Instead, they remained outside the terminal and seemed stressed and vaguely annoyed by the inconvenience of picking her up from the airport. Of course, it didn't mean that they weren't happy to see her! They actually were thrilled but didn't show it in the way she had hoped. She had imagined a version of their lives that didn't match their lived reality—one where they had no other pressures. Similarly, they had likely not imagined what she was anticipating. Because of these kinds of disconnects, our "welcome home scripts" are rarely fulfilled in real life.

If you are honest about what you are expecting, it will make it easier to assign disappointment where it belongs and move on.

▷ Create an honest list of disappointments and joys that you experienced during your sojourn. This is just for yourself, so make it really honest.

▷ Create another list of insights gained now that you've exited the host culture.

▷ Create a list of goals, coping mechanisms, and next steps for your return. This is the last moment of clarity you might have for several months. Use it!

> Because you will be spending a lot of energy on all of this mental processing, be sure to take time to have a little fun and laugh. This is not frivolity, either—you need to balance out your energy with some fun. Be a tourist. You are not in this third culture to engage that culture—it is just a stopover point. Go to a museum, enjoy a park, or visit a landmark. If you drink, it is not a bad time to have a couple of good drinks—but don't get drunk. Hangovers are very counterproductive to the purpose of these few days, and you will almost certainly wish you had this time back.

Upon your actual return to your home culture, anticipate that you will likely experience the stages of culture shock again as you move through reentry shock. For many people, there is an initial euphoria that sets in, although this will often quickly give way to irritability and hostility as people try to relate to the person you were before, rather than the person you are now. If you are welcoming someone back, give them room to express themselves, but don't push for too many details right away.

Coming home is somewhat like walking from a lighted room into a dark room or vice versa—it takes a little time to adjust before you can function. I do not recommend keeping a very ambitious schedule in the first few weeks after returning home, but it is important not to just retreat into your house or room. Here are a few things to expect:

- The intensity and risk factors will again be at play, but differently. For example, thinking of visibility and invisibility, a Peace Corps Volunteer who has become accustomed to being a visible minority in their country of service might have trouble adjusting to the relative anonymity of "fitting in" back home.

- The process of reentry shock is, in my experience, often slightly longer than the experience of culture shock. Moreover, the low is often a little bit lower than it was during culture shock. This means that the feelings of depression and discouragement will again be present. If you continue to process through the experience, this lowness will again be transitory. Six months is not at all unusual for the process of reentry.

- Don't skip the processing! It is very tempting to do whatever it takes to re-assimilate into your home culture, but a failure to adequately process through reentry can cause long-term issues that will crop up at unexpected times. If you need to function at a very high level during this time and find yourself unable to do so, it may be worth consulting a medical or mental health professional. If caused by reentry this is often a transitory issue, but it is important not to avoid dealing with underlying physical or mental health challenges. Remember as well that short-circuiting the processing can be one of the things that would lead to adjustment disorder, as mentioned previously.

▷ Watch out for **shoeboxing**, an idea that originated with Bruce LaBrack, who is one of the leading advocates of reentry training.[34] Essentially, the idea is that it may be tempting to say, "Oh, wasn't that a nice trip," and put all of your memories, souvenirs, pictures, and so on, in a literal or figurative shoebox and set them off to the side. This allows you to revisit them at your leisure, but it does not allow the experience to be reintegrated into your long-term vision of life. Such an approach can lead to what Kiely called a "chameleon with a complex."[35]

▷ Be intentional about coping. Just as in culture shock, the reentry transition can give rise to unhealthy coping mechanisms.

Excessive busyness, irresponsible driving, excessive shopping, misuse of sexuality or relationships, and withdrawal are some of the most common unhealthy coping mechanisms I have seen used. A healthy coping plan and support systems can help you avoid causing long-term problems.

▷ If possible, link in with a support network. If you were on the sojourn with a team, attempt to meet at least once every month for the first six months or so to debrief and catch up with each other. I have seen a real difference between sojourners who have done this and those who haven't. Those who do fare much better. It is also important to use this time to process unresolved relational tensions from the team, if these exist.

▷ Revisit the question of intercultural competence. I suggest taking intercultural competence assessments six months after returning.[36] Taking them earlier than that will often give you results that relate to your transition rather than to your more stable underlying orientations to difference and similarity. Go over these with a coach, consultant, or mentor, and process your experience again.

I have observed that beyond the initial reentry shock, there is also a stage that I call reintegration. This stage can last for several months or even years beyond the initial struggle of reentry, and it involves the quest to integrate lessons learned into your business, education, or cause. This is an important goal, and it is worth reflecting on from time to time to gauge progress.

As friends and family who are welcoming a loved one back from a cross-cultural sojourn, it can be very disconcerting to see the struggles they are going through. Be patient. The worst aspects of culture shock and reentry shock are almost always transitory. Listen. One of the most important things the sojourner needs is a supportive audience. Don't be surprised if you don't understand everything they are talking about or if some of the ideas seem radical to you. This is often just part of the process of trying to figure out what fits where.

NOTES

[34] http://www2.pacific.edu/sis/culture/

[35] Kiely, R. C. (Spring 2004). A Chameleon with a Complex: Searching for Transformation in International Service-Learning. *Michigan Journal of Community Service Learning*.

[36] Find more information about these instruments, at https://iccompetence.traxcultures.com

CHAPTER SEVEN

PARTING WORDS

Whether you are preparing for your first trip abroad, are a seasoned traveler, or a supporter of a sojourner, I hope you have found this guide to be a useful companion. The opportunity to cross cultures can be a great privilege. I urge you to make the most of it by taking the concepts in this book seriously. A few thoughts for specific groups follow.

STUDENTS STUDYING ABROAD

Make the most of your trip by setting intentional goals. One of the biggest limitations you may face is that many times the experience will only facilitate interacting with people from your socioeconomic class. Make an effort to get out into the community and get to know people and their stories. Host family stays are wonderful, but they are most effective when there are a few other people from your own culture that you can interact with.[37] Don't avoid all contact with people who are like you, and at the same time, make sure you have some contact with people who are different from you.

One of the biggest temptations you might face is to simply treat this experience as a resume builder. Be intentional and take the opportunity to develop into a more capable and creative adult.

INTERNATIONAL STUDENTS STUDYING IN THE U.S.

In many cases, there are very high expectations placed on you by yourself, your family, and sometimes your government. It can be very discouraging if you struggle in classes because of the pressure you feel. Access the resources around you. If they are available, access your campus's international student services center and academic support resources. Please understand that if you are from a culture that communicates indirectly, Americans are generally not attuned to this kind of communication. So we might seem insensitive and unhelpful, but often that is not what is intended. I highly recommend that you check out the book *American Ways*.[38] This book will help you understand some of what you are experiencing while you are here. If you can engage the difficulty of learning American culture and really be intentional about recognizing and coping with your culture shock, you will be more likely to have academic success over the course of your studies in the U.S.

MISSIONARIES

Slow down. Most missionaries I know live at such a hectic pace they do not allow themselves room to process. It is not a sign of spiritual weakness to encounter culture shock. It is, instead, a sign that you are human. Practice grace with yourself, your family, and those around you. Missionary anthropologist Paul Hiebert bemoaned the fact that so many missionaries have to deal with culture shock in isolation because of false ideas of what it means to be a good missionary.[39] Pushing through the difficulties of culture shock, although an admirable goal, is foolish. Take the time to process it. Don't think that you won't be faced with your own weakness and darkness. You will. The more you can accept the reality that you need grace, too, the more effective you will be.

PEACE CORPS VOLUNTEERS AND GLOBAL SERVICE LEARNERS[40]

One of the most challenging things you will likely face is the difficulty in reintegrating what you have been learning with life back home. You, more than many others, will likely find reentry and reintegration to be an incredibly trying time. You want to make a difference, and whether or not you have become disillusioned, you are going to find it discouraging that few others understand your perspective on the world. Hang on and journal a lot, because you have a lot to offer the world. At the same time, watch out for the tendency to judge your own culture as particularly bad compared to other cultures (this is called reversal). If you sense this tendency (it is often accompanied by a kind of self-righteous overattachment to another culture), seek out someone who can help you take the Intercultural Development Inventory and process through this. Of course reversal is not limited to these travelers, and every sojourner would do well to watch out for this.

INTERNATIONAL BUSINESSPEOPLE AND BUSINESS TRAVELERS

High-quality international business can not only lead to financial success, it can change the world. Some of the most important things the world needs today can happen through smart business travelers like you. Please take seriously your own need to process your experience. It will, in the end, make you more efficient (not to mention happier). I've heard people say we have a universal business culture. Although this has some merit, there are still massive cultural differences—sometimes just below the surface. Our perceived similarities do not remove the need to be interculturally competent generally, and culturally competent regarding the countries you are working in.

MILITARY MEMBERS

Depending on your branch and specific duties, you may or may not have much direct contact with other cultures. However, I know more and more of you do, as you represent your people abroad. Along with your training, I encourage you to take personal ownership for your transition and the potential experience of culture shock. My own dad and grandfather are both combat veterans, and I know that you and your families go through tremendous (and often repeated) transitions. Use this book, especially Chapter 3, to process through the transitions you are experiencing.

TRAILING SPOUSES[41] AND THIRD-CULTURE KIDS[42]

If you find yourself "along for the ride," your transition may be more difficult than your spouse's or parent's, as his or her time will generally be more structured than yours. Be intentional about your transition process. Having been a third-culture kid, I know how difficult it can be to try to figure out where you are from and how to fit in. As a family, take time to recognize the effects that the cultural transition is having on you. The strain can be significant, so be sure to reaffirm your commitment to each other as part of your coping process.

FAMILY AND FRIENDS OF SOJOURNERS

If you have read this book as a family member or friend of someone going through transition, several pieces of advice. First, be available. Second, don't be surprised if the sojourner you are supporting doesn't act like they need you or want to talk as often as you thought they might. Third, when the person going through transition tells you that everything is horrible, it may be helpful to remember that this is usually only part of the story. Often, you are the safest person they can talk to, and simply verbalizing their frustration is precisely what they need to make it better. Resist the temptation to overreach, but remain a constant presence. Don't be too nosy, but don't be absent. It's a bit of a balancing act, but in the long run, your presence and willingness to listen is what is most valuable.

SPONSORS OF VARIOUS SOJOURNS

If you are a study abroad adviser or program director, a business manager, work in the missions home office, or in some other way are involved with sending people into cross-cultural sojourns, in many ways this book was written for you. You are responsible for the healthy transition of those you send across cultures. You must adequately prepare them for and support them during their sojourn. I emphatically add that you have a moral responsibility to ensure that the sojourner receives adequate reentry support and training upon their return. This is your responsibility—do not shirk it. Moreover, your organization's senior leadership must be aware of and take ultimate responsibility for these principles. A program administrator is relatively powerless to effect high-quality transitions when the organizational system does not support this goal.

CONCLUDING THOUGHTS

I have enjoyed this small journey with you, and I hope you have found this resource to be a helpful one.

Remember, if you are encountering difficulty as you transition across cultures, it is because you are doing something hard. Take good care of yourself and those you care about.

Bon voyage!

NOTES

[37] Vande Berg, M., Paige, R. M., & Lou, K. H. (Eds.). (2012). *Student Learning Abroad: What Our Students Are Learning, What They're Not, and What We Can Do About It.* Sterling, Virginia: Stylus Publishing. More at: https://slabroad.traxcultures.com

[38] Althen, G., & Bennett, J. (2011). *American ways: A cultural guide to the United States* (3rd ed). Boston: Intercultural Press. More at: https://americanways.traxcultures.com

[39] Hiebert, Paul G. (1985). *Anthropological insights for missionaries.* Grand Rapids, MI: Baker Academic. More at: https://anthformiss.traxcultures.com

[40] Jones, S. W. (2011). Intercultural development in global service-learning (Master's Thesis, University of the Pacific). https://intcldevglobalsl.traxcultures.com

[41] Harvey, M. (1998). Dual-career couples during international relocation: The trailing spouse. The International Journal of Human Resource Management, 9(2), 309–331. https://doi.org/10.1080/095851998341116

[42] Pollock, D. C., Van Reken, R. E., & Pollock, M. V. (2017). Third culture kids: Growing up among worlds (3rd edition). Boston, MA: Nicholas Brealey Pub. More at: https://thirdculture.traxcultures.com

GLOSSARY

agency: a sense of both responsibility and empowerment in relation to one's situation.

ambivalence: an inability to make decisions, wherein multiple options seem equally possible or equally disinteresting.

apathy: a sense of not caring, often accompanied by an inability to engage one's environment, even to one's own detriment.

bureaucracy: the official systems that an organization or government uses to accomplish its business. In the international setting, bureaucracy is usually confusing to people from other cultures (and sometimes to people who live there as well). The process of navigating a bureaucracy to accomplish something like renewing a visa or paying your power bill can be very frustrating, especially in countries without a high value on efficiency.

coping: refers to the way in which people try to deal with difficult circumstances. Sometimes people cope by removing the difficulty, or by removing themselves from the situation in which the difficulty is occurring. However, it is often not possible to completely escape the stressor, which in turn requires people to develop ways to deal with the ongoing stress. Some of these ways are healthy, or adaptive, while others are destructive, or maladaptive.

culture shock: the effects of cumulative disorientation that come from extended contact with another culture, often proceeding in three stages: emotional high, disenchantment or discouragement, and developing confidence.

culture: according to Milton Bennett, culture is the learned and shared values, beliefs, and behaviors of a group of interacting people. More simply, culture is *how people do their stuff together.*

cumulative disorientation: the primary cause of culture shock, the result of extended exposure to another culture, in which a person's "map" of how the world works is repeatedly violated by the host culture.

disenchantment: the stage of culture shock during which a sojourner discovers that the host culture and the experience overall are not as fun or positive as they originally seemed. This is often accompanied by a growing realization of the sojourner's own ineptitude in the host culture.

disintegration: a growing incapacity to function. This can look like having trouble getting out of bed, difficulty relating to coworkers, inability to accomplish tasks, or even unusual outbursts of emotion. Often the most distressing thing about disintegration is that you discover that something you were once good at is now extremely difficult. This is almost always a passing stage, but it is deeply disturbing.

elevator speech: a short (often 30 seconds or less) summary of your experience, designed to gauge how interested your listener is in finding out more about your experience. It should be concise enough that you could share the entire speech during an elevator ride.

emotional high: often the first stage of culture shock, in which a person experiences an often illogical enjoyment of the host culture and tends to interpret the world (especially the host culture) through an overwhelmingly positive lens.

endings: the first stage of transition, in which things which were once true about a person are no longer true or applicable due to the transition.

expat: someone who is living out of his or her home country (also called the passport country).

expectations: the often-unstated assumptions about what will (or what should) happen. While expectations are not bad, they are most helpful when they are acknowledged, because they often will not be fulfilled, or at least not in the ways you anticipate.

frames for understanding: sometimes called worldview; includes many different areas of knowing. Frames for understanding are the (usually culturally generated) explanations that we use for comprehending both simple and complex phenomena.

frame shifting: the capacity to move back and forth between different cultures' frames; to approximate taking another perspective.

global nomad: a person who for one reason or another does not have a permanent home and who generally lives in one country only for a few years at a time before moving on. For a few, this is a lifestyle choice. For some, this is the reality required by the profession the person is in. This can lead to a sense of being a global citizen on the one hand, and to a sense of rootlessness on the other.

global: referring to a way of seeing the world that acknowledges that there are many different perspectives. While this idea does not require that you agree with other perspectives, it does imply that you understand these perspectives make sense to the people who hold them. For example, you might not agree with indirect communication as the best way to communicate, but with a global mindset, you are able to understand that some people have really legitimate reasons for thinking it is the best way to communicate.

homesickness: an experience of profoundly missing one's home, especially family and friends. Homesickness is not limited to cultural transitions, but it is often especially profound when the ability to return home is further limited by geographic distance.

honeymoon stage: another way to describe the *emotional high* at the beginning of culture shock.

intensity factors: the features of a cross-cultural experience that make it more difficult, especially psychologically.

intercultural competence: can be used to refer to various measures of how effective a person is at functioning across cultures. One of the most important ways to define intercultural competence is in relation to a person's ability to accurately understand and relate to both cultural difference and cultural similarity—a mode of competence that is measured by the Intercultural Development Inventory. Other measures of intercultural competence focus on resiliency, adaptation, and similar interactions between a person and his or her social and physical environments.[43]

jet lag: extreme tiredness cause by travel, such as by airplane, and especially by rapidly changing multiple time zones. This is especially pronounced when "flipping" the day and night as a result of literally ending up on the other side of the world. The effects of jet lag can last more than a week and can cause impaired judgement.

journaling: a process used for recording one's experiences and thoughts. Especially useful for critical reflection. Blogging also can be useful, although for many people a physical journal seems to be more useful for sorting out difficult personal issues brought to the fore by transitions.

linguistic competence: refers to the ability to accurately understand and communicate in a language, especially including listening, speaking, reading, and writing. There are various measures of linguistic competence, but it has been estimated that it takes ten years to become fluent in a target language, meaning that there are no significant gaps (especially in expressions and specialized vocabulary).

monocultural: held in contrast to global, a person with a monocultural mindset can only acknowledge his or her own culture's perspective on the way the world works. Not only is the person's culture the right way to understand the world, but it's really the only way.

neutral zone: see *transition zone*.

new beginnings: the final stage of transition, in which a person's identity begins to reorganize and incorporate new elements which were not previously experienced.

reentry shock: refers to the intense psychological discomfort that accompanies returning home after a significant cross-cultural experience. This is very similar to culture shock, and it often follows the same pattern, although it can last longer and can even be more difficult than culture shock.

risk factors: the elements of an experience that increase the feeling of risk, especially psychologically.

role deprivation: in relation to cultural transition, refers to the lack of opportunity to be recognized in roles familiar to you. Causes of this discomfort can include: the roles themselves don't exist in the new context, because they are perceived differently, or because you are not perceived to be the sort of person who fills those roles.

self-awareness: the extent to which you recognize how you function and how you are perceived by others. On the one hand, self-awareness is a very useful trait for success across cultures. On the other hand, it can be uncomfortable to realize how you come across. Additionally, an extreme self-awareness can keep you from actually engaging with other people and can thus be debilitating.

shoeboxing: packing up all of your memories associated with a cross-cultural sojourn into a literal or metaphorical shoebox, only accessing them from time to time. This is held in contrast to integrating lessons and insights from the sojourn into your life.

sojourner: a person who is away from home, generally in another country, and often with some purpose for the travel, such as business, study, or exploration.

tacit knowledge: the things that we know without having to acknowledge that we know them—the knowledge in the back of our minds.

third-culture kid (TCK): a kid growing up in a culture which is neither his nor that of his parents. At the same time, he is not a member of the host culture. Thus, he is in between his home (or passport) culture, and his host (or adoptive) culture. Because he is not a member of either culture, he is called a third-culture kid. Common examples are missionary kids, military kids, and diplomats' kids.

thread of continuity: those elements of a person which remain constant before, during, and after a transition, even if they are not necessarily experienced as constant by the person undergoing transition.

transition zone: the middle stage of a transition, during which a person's identity is particularly challenged by the transition. It is often difficult to gain traction during this time. Also called the neutral zone.

NOTES

[43] For a comprehensive description, see Bennett, M. J. (2013). *Basic concepts of intercultural communication: Paradigms, principles, & practice: selected readings* (Second Edition). Boston: Intercultural Press, A Nicholas Brealey Pub. Company. For more see: https://basicconcepts.traxcultures.com

ADDITIONAL RESOURCES

Basic Concepts of Intercultural Communication
by Milton J. Bennett
https://basicconcepts.traxcultures.com

Communicating Across Cultures
by Stella Ting-Toomey and Tenzin Dorjee
https://commacross.traxcultures.com

Doing Member Care Well
by Kelly O'Donnell
https://membercare.traxcultures.com

Handbook of Intercultural Training
by Dan Landis, Janet M. Bennett, and Milton J. Bennett
https://handbook.traxcultures.com

Race Ethnicity and Self
by Elizabeth Pathy Salett and Diane R. Koslow
https://raceandself.traxcultures.com

Returning Well
Melissa Chaplin
https://returningwell.traxcultures.com

The Art of Coming Home
by Craig Storti
https://cominghome.traxcultures.com

The Art of Crossing Cultures
by Craig Storti
https://crossing.traxcultures.com

Third Culture Kids
by David C. Pollock, Ruth E. Van by Reken, and Michael V. Pollock
https://thirdculture.traxcultures.com

REFERENCES

Althen, G., & Bennett, J. (2011). *American ways: A cultural guide to the United States* (3rd ed). Boston: Intercultural Press.

Bennett, M. J. (2013). *Basic concepts of intercultural communication: Paradigms, principles, & practice: selected readings* (Second Edition). Boston: Intercultural Press, A Nicholas Brealey Pub. Company.

Bennett, M. J. (2013, September 28). The ravages of reification: Considering the iceberg and cultural intelligence, Towards de-reifying intercultural competence. Presented at the FILE IV, Colle Val d'Elsa, Italy. Retrieved from http://www.idrinstitute.org/allegati/IDRI_t_Pubblicazioni/77/FILE_Documento_Intercultura_Reification.pdf

Bridges, William. (2004). *Transitions: Making sense of life's changes.* (2nd Ed.). Cambridge, MA: DeCapo.

Central Office for Foreign Education. (n.d.). Retrieved December 8, 2019, from https://www.kmk.org/zab/central-office-for-foreign-education.html

Covey, S. R. (2013). *The 7 habits of highly effective people: Powerful lessons in personal change* (25th anniversary edition). New York: Simon & Schuster.

Emerson, R. M., Fretz, R. I., & Shaw, L. L. (1995). Writing Ethnographic Fieldnotes (1st ed.). University Of Chicago Press.

Fitzpatrick, F. (2017). Taking the "culture" out of "culture shock"—a critical review of literature on cross-cultural adjustment in international relocation. Critical Perspectives on International Business, 13(4), 278–296. https://doi.org/10.1108/cpoib-01-2017-0008

Furnham, A. (2019). Culture Shock: A Review of the Literature for Practitioners. *Psychology*, *10*, 1832. https://doi.org/10.4236/psych.2019.1013119

Furnham, A., & Bochner, S. (1986). *Culture shock: Psychological reactions to unfamiliar environments.* London ; New York: Methuen.

Goldstein, S. B., & Keller, S. R. (2015). U.S. college students' lay theories of culture shock. International Journal of Intercultural Relations, 47, 187–194.

Harvey, M. (1998). Dual-career couples during international relocation: The trailing spouse. The International Journal of Human Resource Management, 9(2), 309–331. https://doi.org/10.1080/095851998341116

Hiebert, Paul G. (1985). *Anthropological insights for missionaries.* Grand Rapids, MI: Baker Academic.

Hoffman, E. (1990). *Lost in Translation: A Life in a New Language.* Penguin.

Hughes, L. (1993). The Big Sea: An Autobiography (2nd Hill and Wang ed). New York: Hill and Wang. p. 103.

Jones, S. W. (2011). Intercultural development in global service-learning (Master's Thesis, University of the Pacific).

Kiely, R. C. (Spring 2004). A Chameleon with a Complex: Searching for Transformation in International Service-Learning. *Michigan Journal of Community Service Learning*.

Kohls, Robert L. (2001). *Survival kit for overseas living: For Americans planning to live and work abroad.* (4th Ed.). Boston, MA: Nicholas Brealey.

Lucas, J. (2009). Over-stressed, Overwhelmed, and Over Here: Resident Directors and the Challenges of Student Mental Health Abroad. *Frontiers: The Interdisciplinary Journal of Study Abroad, XVIII,* 187–216.

Morrison, T., & Conaway, W. A. (2006). Kiss, bow, or shake hands: The bestselling guide to doing business in more than 60 countries (2nd ed). Avon, Mass: Adams Media.

Oberg, K. (1960). Cultural Shock: Adjustment to New Cultural Environments. Practical Anthropology, os-7(4), 177–182. https://doi.org/10.1177/009182966000700405

Paige, R. M., Cohen, A. D., Kappler, B., Chi, J. C., & Lassegard, J. P. (2006). Maximizing Study Abroad a Student's Guide to Strategies for Language and Culture Learning and Use (2nd ed.). Board of Regents University of Minnesota.

Paige, R. Michael. (1993). "On the nature of intercultural experiences and intercultural education." *Education for the intercultural experience.* (2nd Ed.). Edited by R. Michael Paige. Yarmouth, ME: Intercultural Press.

Pollock, D. C., Van Reken, R. E., & Pollock, M. V. (2017). Third culture kids: Growing up among worlds (3rd edition). Boston, MA: Nicholas Brealey Pub.

Presbitero, A. (2016). Culture shock and reverse culture

shock: The moderating role of cultural intelligence in international students' adaptation. International Journal of Intercultural Relations, 53, 28–38. https://doi.org/10.1016/j.ijintrel.2016.05.004

Putz, L. E., Schmitz, J., & Walch, K. (2014). *Maximizing Business Results with the Strategic Performance Framework: The Cultural Orientations Guide* (6th Edition). Princeton, N.J.: TMC: A Berlitz Company.

Vande Berg, M., Paige, R. M., & Lou, K. H. (Eds.). (2012). *Student Learning Abroad: What Our Students Are Learning, What They're Not, and What We Can Do About It.* Sterling, Virginia: Stylus Publishing.

Ward, C., Bochner, S., & Furnham, A. (2001). *The Psychology of Culture Shock* (2nd ed.).

ABOUT THE AUTHOR

Stephen W. Jones has a diverse disciplinary background including business, intercultural relations, international security, political science, and ministry. He is a Ph.D. Candidate in International Development at the University of Southern Mississippi. Jones is Assistant Professor of International Studies at Crown College in Minnesota, where he teaches International Relations and Intercultural Youth Development. He has led students on learning experiences in Africa, Asia, Europe, Latin America, and North America. Jones is a husband, father, professor, and friend.

www.ingramcontent.com/pod-product-compliance
Lightning Source LLC
Chambersburg PA
CBHW072022110526
44592CB00012B/1402